T0155246

# Free-Format RPG IV
## *Third Edition*

## Jim Martin

MC Press Online, LLC
Boise, ID 83703  USA

**Free-Format RPG IV, Third Edition**

*Jim Martin*

Third Edition

© Copyright 2015 Jim Martin. All rights reserved.

**MC Press Online, LLC**
*Corporate Offices:* 3695 W. Quail Heights Court, Boise, ID 83703-3861 USA
*Sales and Customer Service:* (208) 629-7275 ext. 500;
service@mcpressonline.com
*Permissions and Bulk/Special Orders:* mcbooks@mcpressonline.com
www.mcpressonline.com • www.mc-store.com

ISBN: 978-1-58347-413-6                                    EB201505

*To my lovely wife Jody,*
*for her encouragement and support in all that I pursue*

# Acknowledgments

I wish to express my appreciation to several people who have encouraged me over many years.

Thanks to Dave Michelson, my mentor and friend; to Phil Bolian, who inspired me to pursue excellence; to professor Herb Morris of Bradley University, who taught me well and fueled the fire of interest in computer science; to Kathy Thorpe, who gave me opportunities to learn and grow; to Bill Merchantz, who coached me as a new manager; and to Victoria and Katie at MC Press, who have taken my vision and turned it into a reality.

My thanks also go to my friend Joe Pluta, who kindly provided technical assistance in the programming-language comparison section of this book.

# Contents

# Preface to the Third Edition

This third edition of *Free-Format RPG IV* has come quickly on the heels of the second edition—to provide you with the best organizational content and updates after recent enhancements to the RPG IV programming language for IBM i® systems.

Free-format RPG now encompasses nearly all functional aspects of the language: H (control), F (file definitions), D (definitions), C (calculations), and P (subprocedures). It's easier now to state which RPG functions are *not* free-format: program-described files and I (input) and O (output) specifications. This edition not only explains the new features—it uses them throughout the book, in all examples.

The addition of free-format control, file, definition, and procedure specifications has propelled RPG into a relevant modern programming language. With these latest changes, it was IBM's goal to make RPG easier to learn for newcomers, and also easy for long-term RPG programmers to learn and use. I believe they have accomplished this goal.

Since there is no longer a need for the /Free compiler directive, my fear is that RPG procedures will become a sloppy mixture of old and new syntax. Prior editions of this book expressed my view that mixing formats is not a good practice.

RPG IV now has a new lease on life and provides us with the capabilities we need going forward. Don't you wonder sometimes—what's next?

*Jim Martin*
*January 2015*

# A Note About Source Entry

Program source entry on IBM i is changing. For a very long time, we used Source Entry Utility (SEU). SEU came with the operating system, as part of a utilities package. When the PC became a commonly used terminal (thanks to 5250 emulation software), IBM introduced an "SEU-like" program called CODE/400 (eventually just CODE). With this product, you connected to the system and requested the program you wanted to edit. From that point on, you edited off-line, using a graphical interface, and sent the revised program back to the system when you were finished editing. Although CODE was used by many, it did not replace SEU for most users of the system.

A few years ago, IBM's WebSphere® group came up with a new editor as part of a product called WebSphere Development Studio Client (WDSc). In this case, client meant a PC. Within this product, the Remote System Explorer (RSE) used an editor called LPEX, which stands for *Li*ve *P*arsing *EX*tensible editor. Many programmers loved this new graphical editor, but although the cost was low, the PC needed to be large (in terms of main storage and speed) at the time.

Fast forward a few years to when IBM enhanced and repackaged the RSE/LPEX product within a new product called Rational Developer for System i (RDi). Separate from IBM i, the product now was licensed by user. A few years later, along came the Power® systems, and RDi was rechristened RDp: Rational Developer for Power. Then, a year or so ago, the name reverted back to RDi. So today, its name is RDi.

Again, many programmers embraced the new graphical interface to source program entry. To encourage the user community to convert to the new product, IBM stopped enhancements to SEU at V6R1. As a consequence, the V7.1 enhancements to RPG IV are reflected back to SEU users as syntax errors. So, if you are an SEU user (and many are), you will have to ignore the SEU error messages when entering V7 (and beyond) enhancements and override the return to editing option (from Y to N) when exiting an SEU session. The compiler will tell you if you have made errors in source entry.

I would be less than honest if I didn't mention one of the reasons why SEU users have been slow to adopt RDi/RSE/LPEX: It has been fairly expensive. I contacted IBM and received the following price quote:

> The current price for IBM Rational Developer for i RPG & COBOL Tools Floating User Single Install Initial Fixed Term License plus Software Subscription and Support for 12 Months is $835.

And the price will still vary depending on many factors. You will need to contact IBM to get a firm quote.

Also, some training may be needed to learn how to use this new software properly. RDi is a robust product, and it contains more than just a source entry capability. Consider attending breakout sessions on RDi at a COMMON conference or an RPG & DB2 Summit conference.

A book that has helped me is *The Remote System Explorer* (MC Press, 2008) by Don Yantzi and Nazmin Haji of the IBM Rational Developer lab that developed and supports the RDi product.

# 1

# Pre–Free-Format RPG IV

The RPG programming language has certainly come a long way since its introduction as a simple report program generator in the 1960s. From the earliest versions of RPG to the latest release of free-format RPG IV on the IBM® Power® platform, the changes have been dramatic.

The centerpiece of today's RPG is its support for a free-format style of coding. Free format puts RPG on the map of modern programming languages and gives programmers important functionality for constructing programs that are easier to create, understand, and maintain. If you are writing RPG programs today, you owe it to yourself to make the most of this great function.

In this book, you will learn the ins and outs of free-format RPG, from coding file definitions, data structures and other definitions, I/O, and program flow to data manipulation, math operations, and call and return. But before we dive into the delights of free-format RPG, let's take a brief look at its precursor: fixed-format RPG IV.

## RPG IV

Even before free format, RPG IV was a powerful, functionally rich programming language. RPG IV—or ILE RPG, as it is officially known—debuted in late 1994 with Version 3 Release 1 (V3R1) of the IBM i® operating system. IBM had introduced the Integrated Language Environment® (ILE) in a prior release, but everyone eagerly awaited RPG's entrée into ILE. Three major additions to RPG in V3R1 brought the language a significant level of sophistication that was absent before: the extended Factor 2, built-in functions, and subprocedures.

## Extended Factor 2

The introduction of the extended Factor 2 format, along with operations to exploit it, represented a huge departure from RPG's past. With this enhancement to calculation specifications, RPG programmers could now use operations such as Eval (Evaluate expression) and If (If) with long expressions.

The ability to use math symbols (+, –, *, /) within expressions was a major step in modernizing the language. Other symbols, used in comparison expressions, included equal (=), less than (<), greater than (>), less than or equal (<=), greater than or equal (>=), and not equal (<>). The exponentiation symbol (**) became the newest math operator, and support for parentheses let programmers indicate higher precedence in math or comparison expressions. Other programming languages had used these symbols for a while, and IBM chose to bring them into its new version of RPG.

One of the symbols, the plus operator (+), also found another use in RPG IV: concatenation. Using this new operator, programmers could put character data together into strings much more easily than with previous methods.

## Built-in Functions

Programmers were already familiar with built-in functions through their use of such functions in OS/400 Control Language (CL). The %Sst (Substring) and %Bin (Binary) functions, for example, are commonly used CL built-in functions.

The whole idea of an RPG IV built-in function was based on the C language function idea. A built-in function performs one task, with or without parameters, and usually returns data of a predetermined data type to the point in the program where the function was specified. For example, RPG IV's %Eof (End-of-file) built-in function checks for end of file after a Read operation, eliminating the need to code a resulting indicator on the Read. The %Found built-in function lets you check for a record-found condition after a Chain operation without using a resulting indicator.

The number of built-in functions available in RPG, as of V7.1 of IBM i, has grown from the dozen or so in RPG IV's initial release to 80 now. Many of these built-in functions duplicate the function of older operation codes, such as Scan (built-in function %Scan) and Substr (built-in function %Subst). In some cases, the built-in function provides more capabilities than the operation code it replaces. For example, the %Subst (Get substring) built-in function can substring a target string as well as a source string, whereas the Subst operation code can substring only a source string.

## Subprocedures

As if these new capabilities weren't enough, IBM added another big feature to RPG IV. Subprocedures give RPG IV programmers the option to break complex programs into smaller parts and to create "homegrown" built-in functions if desired. For the first time in RPG, the concept of a "local" variable was introduced for use in subprocedures. Also for the first time, a routine—in this case, a subprocedure—was able to use recursion.

# Other Changes

In RPG IV, IBM also eliminated many of the old constraints of RPG IV's predecessor, RPG/400®. Eight-character file and record names were lengthened to 10. Field names were lengthened, too—at first to 10 and then to 4,096! The maximum size of character fields was enlarged from 256 bytes to 16 megabytes! Packed numeric field length size was raised to 30 and then 31 digits; it now stands at 63.

Even fans of binary and hexadecimal programming were given something new in RPG IV. Previously, you could convert two-byte binary numbers to four-digit decimal numbers and convert four-byte binary numbers to nine digits. The new RPG IV language provided an integer data type, both signed and unsigned, up to 20 digits. To handle ultra-small and ultra-large numbers, the floating-point data type made its debut, in both standard and double precision.

Other data types added to the language include the pointer data type, which contains the address of data or a procedure; the date, time, and timestamp data types; and the object data type, used to handle references to a Java® object.

Adding these new data types and enlarging the older ones must have come from some larger motivating factor. Why did IBM provide all these things? In my opinion, the reasons lie in maintaining the Power system as a modern and viable solution for the midrange server marketplace. Older RPG can easily be called a "dinosaur" in this modern age. The gap in programming capabilities between older RPG and modern languages such as C, C++, Java, and others is huge. With today's RPG IV, there is no gap. RPG IV has "come from behind" to be a major player in the modern world of application development.

## Some "Baggage" That Came Along

Like any responsible vendor, IBM doesn't like to offend any of its customers. If you wrote an RPG program in 1969 that used the RPG cycle and 99 indicators, IBM won't tell you that your approach is obsolete. Instead, IBM continues to provide a compatibility path from the "here and now" back to almost any previous time in RPG's history. The machines may change every six to eight years, but programs and the inherent investment made in developing them are preserved.

One byproduct of this commitment to long-time customers and their legacy code is that RPG IV, in its current form, carries the weight of 40 years of "baggage." The RPG cycle, and its emulation of 1960s accounting machines, lives on.

When IBM introduced RPG IV, many of us hoped we might see a break with the past. Companies that cared little about change could stay with RPG/400, and those interested in new ideas could embrace the new incarnation of RPG. Maybe, I thought, the new RPG would at least drop the cycle. Perhaps we'd be able to use only newer instructions—such as Eval—with oldies like ADD, SUB, MULT, and DIV relegated to the history books. Maybe calculation "definitions" would be eliminated in light of the new definition specifications.

But, no, we got all the older operations and functions along with the new. Today's RPG IV truly is a huge collage of language functionality, encompassing both old and new functions!

New programs don't have to use the old operation codes, primary files, or variables defined in calculations. All this is true. But did you know that a kernel of the RPG cycle code is a part of every RPG IV program, even if you did not specify a primary file? How else could the LR and RT indicators do their jobs?

## The Future

In Chapter 2, I explain why I believe that the free-format style is a better alternative to coding RPG IV. In fact, I will go so far as to say that this new style is necessary for the future of this programming language. The chapters that follow introduce you to free-format RPG IV and then delve into the details, providing plenty of examples to demonstrate the features of the language. Here's a preview of some of the good news: In a major break with the past, most of the original-format operations aren't available in free-format RPG.

Modern programmers see the free-format style as RPG's newfound strength. There will always be some who will criticize IBM for omitting a preferred language function in free format. Regardless, free-format RPG IV is a great, modern programming language!

# 2

# The Case
# for Free-Format RPG

We in the RPG community can gain important advantages by adopting the free-format style of coding. There will always be RPG programmers who prefer to code using the fixed-format method, and that is fine. My goal in writing this chapter is to describe some of the benefits to be reaped if you embrace the free-format style.

## Easier to Read and Maintain

The greatest advantage that free-format RPG IV offers you as a programmer is that it lets you write code that is easier to read and maintain. The great majority of RPG IV programmers today are maintenance programmers. As a maintenance programmer, you inherit programs written by someone else. If a program is written well, with lots of comments and a clear structure, the job of fixing or changing it isn't too bad. The quality of the original program, more than your own abilities, is what determines productivity.

A program that is easier to read is easier to maintain. What makes a program "easier to read?" That's an interesting question, which I will now try to answer.

A program is easier to read if the author of the program observed the following practices:

- Good field naming
- Indenting
- Use of comments
- No Goto operations

Free-format RPG IV offers us an opportunity to implement each of these programming practices.

## Good Field Naming

The six-character field names of RPG/400 are over. Fixed or free, we in RPG IV can now use longer names, and we should. Granted, DDS still restricts us to 10-character names, but that is not nearly as bad as six.

The problem with short names is that they force us to be cryptic, and "cryptic" is the antithesis of good field naming. The name-length limit is now huge at 4,096 positions, enabling us to create names that aid the reader in understanding what is happening in a program. Names that are too long can be just as miserable as names that are too short, so I suggest a happy middle ground around 10 to 15 characters long.

In addition to having an appropriate length, field names should be meaningful. That's easier said than done, I know, but we must try. Which of these two field names is more meaningful: TOTAL or Month_Sales_Total?

The principles of good field naming apply to indicators, too. In RPG IV, we can name our indicators. In fact, an unlimited number of named indicators are available to us. The jury is in on numbered indicators. They are cryptic and no longer necessary in RPG IV, for any reason. If you saw the following code in an RPG program that you had been assigned to maintain, what would you need to do first?

```
If      *In67
   .
   .
   .
Endif
```

You would need to find out what *IN67 means! To determine where this indicator was used and changed, you would need to use the compiler cross-reference.

By their very nature, numbered indicators are cryptic. It takes time to unravel their meaning. In larger programs, an indicator may serve more than one purpose. Decrypting these situations takes even more time.

Naming indicators isn't a new idea. Named fields defined as Boolean (e.g.,*LGL in CL) have been around for decades in other programming languages. What if we substituted a well-named named indicator in the preceding code example?

```
If      Over_CR_Limit
  .
  .
  .
Endif
```

For a maintenance programmer, it is far more productive to make program changes or fixes when the program uses indicators like this one. As with field names, choosing a good name for the indicator is important. Names such as Flag_1, Flag_2, and so on are no better than *IN67.

For indicators associated with externally described files, use the named indicator data structure, with file description keyword INDDS. You also must specify file-level keyword INDARA on the external file's DDS to permit this feature to be compiled properly. If an indicator in a display file has two meanings, depending on which record format is being used, just create two entries for the same indicator in the data structure. Even the overflow indicator associated with external printer files can be a standalone named indicator.

The availability of longer names helps us make programs easier to read. Using such names in fixed format's extended Factor 2 area is fine, but the available space is limited to positions 36–80, or 45 locations. In free format, the line space available for an operation and its parameters is positions 8–80, or 73 locations. Even allowing for an operation code, that gives you approximately 50 percent more room to enter field names and expression operators.

Long expressions that include longer names will look "crowded" in the extended Factor 2 format. Free format eliminates (to some extent) this problem.

## Indenting

When you indent your code, you give readers of your program visual cues about your intent as the program's author. We use indenting in data structures to clarify for the reader what the data structure subfields are. We do the same thing for parameters in prototypes and procedure interface definitions.

Indenting calculations wasn't possible in RPG until free format became available. A common practice for maintenance programmers faced with a complex nesting of If and Do groups has been to print out the complex section, tape the pages together (if not using continuous forms), and then use a ruler and pen to "bracket" the Ifs and Dos. The purpose of this bracketing is to provide a visual aid in understanding the logic. I've certainly performed this exercise many times.

In free-format RPG IV, you can indent statements that lie within an If or Do block. By indenting, you create a visual aid to help the maintenance programmers who will come later understand the program logic better. Other free-format languages, including C, Cobol, Pascal, PL/1, and others, have used this approach for years. Indenting, like good field naming, helps make programs easier to read and maintain.

## Use of Comments

Any program is easier to understand and maintain if the program author chooses to use comments. Including comments in your programs takes a bit of extra time when coding, but it yields a big savings in time for the maintenance programmer. It is naive to assume that maintenance programmers can read and understand others' programs quickly, especially very large programs. Having plenty of good comments really helps.

"How much should I comment?" I hear this question all the time, and I have a stock response: "As much as you have time for." An investment in comments yields a great reward later on.

In fixed-format RPG IV, you can specify comments almost anywhere in a program by placing an asterisk (*) in position 7. The entire line is then considered a comment. On a calculation line, comments are permitted in positions 81–100. If you are using a traditional 24x80 display, you cannot see these "end-line" comments unless you either scroll to the right or use the alternate display format, which shows 27 lines and 132 columns. I am not a big fan of the alternate display format because the screen data then becomes very small and harder to see.

In free-format RPG IV, you can enter a comment on any line by preceding it with two forward slashes (//). The slashes can begin in position 8 to provide a complete line of comment. Comments can also appear at the end of a line of source code. Free-format specifications end in position 80, so all comments are viewable using the traditional 24x80 display. In free-format RPG, you may continue comments up to position 100; however, if you do so, you run the risk of their not being seen or updated when changes are made in the code.

Because most lines of code in free format use only a small portion of the available space, an opportunity arises to include a fairly long comment on the *same line* as the calculation operation and its parameters. Placing a comment on the same line as the associated code reduces confusion on the part of the program reader. In fixed format, longer comments must come either before or after the calculation line or be lost in positions 81–100.

In free-format RPG IV, then, we need fewer lines of code to provide the actual program operations *and* the comments, with less confusion. Free format's comment support helps make our programs easier to read and maintain.

## No Goto Operations

Nothing strikes fear in the heart of a maintenance programmer faster than the sight of a Goto operation in a program. The thought of unraveling a complex maze of logic as the program jumps from one point to another and then back is very unsettling. The program lacks proper structure.

Studies have shown that Goto operations are unnecessary in well-structured programs. In RPG IV, whether fixed- or free-format, loop interrupters are available. The Iter (Iterate) operation "jumps" to the next Enddo or Endfor; the Leave (Leave a Do/For group) operation jumps to the next instruction after the Enddo or Endfor; and the LeaveSr (Leave a subroutine) operation jumps out of the subroutine within which it occurs.

Free-format RPG IV provides no support for the Goto operation, forcing programmers to use structured operations to accomplish program objectives. Without Goto, our programs are easier to read and maintain.

## Conclusions

If you follow the programming practices I have described—good field naming, named indicators, prolific comments, indented calculation logic sections, and no Goto operations—your programs will take on a good style that is easy to read and maintain. This approach provides a financial payback as well. If maintenance programming accounts for 80 percent of the total cost of an application, improving the productivity and efficiency of the maintenance-programming operations can yield real financial gains. In a large organization, you might need fewer programmers. In a smaller organization, you might be able to postpone hiring additional staff. Making programs easier to read and maintain translates into "people" cost savings and lets you do more with less, due to increased productivity.

# A "Modern" Programming Style

In providing support for free-format operations and expressions, IBM has given the RPG language some capabilities that you will find in today's most popular programming languages. Today's RPG is a stronger, more flexible, more intuitive language, thanks to features such as built-in functions, new data types, indented logic, and an improved procedure call mechanism. Big differences will always exist among the capabilities of different programming languages, but free-format RPG IV calculation operations are surprisingly similar to some of the other modern languages available today.

## Free-Format RPG IV and C

Consider the following program segment, written in free-format RPG IV. The code performs a bubble sort of an array. In this code, n is the number of elements in the array, and i and j are indexes.

```
For i = 1 to n;        // Outer loop
 For j = 1 to n-1;  // Inner loop
   If Array(j+1) < Array(j);  // Out of order?
     SaveElem   = Array(j);     // Yes - swap elements
     Array(j)   = Array(j+1); // |
     Array(j+1) = SaveElem;   // |
   Endif;
 Endfor;
Endfor;
```

Now, take a look at the equivalent routine written in C:

```
for(i = 0; i < n; i++)
   for(j = 0; j < n-1; j++)
      if(Array[j+1]  <  Array[j]) {
         SaveElem  = Array[j];
         Array[j]    = Array[j+1];
         Array[j+1] = SaveElem;
         }
```

Other than some minor syntactical differences, the two routines are identical. To be sure, RPG IV handles I/O differently than C does, and C uses null-terminated character strings (arrays) rather than a character field with a length. Also, C uses integer and float data types primarily for numeric operations, while RPG mostly uses decimal (but fully supports integer and float). C uses functions with return values, and RPG IV uses subprocedures with return values. C passes variables to called programs by value; RPG IV can pass parameters by value or by reference.

In spite of these obvious differences, free-format RPG still has a look and feel similar to the C language.

## *Free-Format RPG IV and Java*

Now, compare the RPG IV routine with the equivalent routine written in a Java method:

```
for (i=0; i<n; i++) {            // outer loop
   for(j=0; j<n-i-1; j++) {      // inner loop
      if(array[j+1] < array[j]) {  // out of order?
         SaveElem = Array[j];      // swap elements
         Array[j]  = Array[j+1];
         Array[j+1] = SaveElem;
      }
   }
}
```

Huge differences in functionality exist between these two languages. Java is an object-oriented language; RPG IV is not. Java is a great graphical interface language, but RPG IV is not. RPG IV is a great database-handling language, but Java is not. Nevertheless, the differences in look and feel between the two languages are once again minor.

## *Conclusions*

As this comparison of programming code demonstrates, the language syntax of free-format RPG IV isn't so different from other modern programming languages. Free format thus eases the "learning curve" transition both to and from these other languages.

Each programming language has different capabilities, and each has its own strengths and weaknesses. Rather than choose one language to do everything needed in a Power development organization, we should use the best language for the job. For most business functions, RPG IV is an excellent choice. For graphical interface requirements, many organizations look to Java. C provides extensive mathematical and other functions not available in RPG IV. RPG IV can interface easily with programs written in these other languages, providing a way to integrate the strengths of each language.

# Being "Current"

Free-format RPG has been available for many years now. Its acceptance as a viable alternative to the fixed-format style is fairly well accepted now. One need that free-format RPG IV satisfies is the desire on the part of both programmers and managers to maintain "current" skills.

## *The Programmer's Perspective*

My work has taken me to a wide variety of companies and many Power/System i user groups. I see programmers on a daily basis. A common thread that I have observed among these programmers is the desire to be better than they are now and to stay current with the capabilities of the programming language that they are using. Changes to RPG IV have come fast and furious in recent years. Staying on top of the latest capabilities will continue to be a challenge, requiring seekers to consult books, speakers at conferences, Internet newsletters, and even the programmer in the next cubicle.

My experience with most RPG programmers is that they really love their jobs. They enjoy trying out new functions and seeing how they work. RPG programmers are creative, and they take pride in the fact that their creations are being used day-to-day to run a business. RPG programmers want to keep doing what they already know well. Staying current is one way to become more efficient in their jobs, opening the doors of opportunity to career growth within their current organizations. If a job change is either required or wanted, knowledge of and experience with RPG's latest capabilities is highly desirable.

## Management's Perspective

Programmers who possess current skills help solve one of IT management's biggest concerns: the ability of staff to do the programming work, to do it well, and to do it efficiently. At this point in history, the "people" cost is the biggest portion of the expense involved in producing and maintaining computer applications. Getting and keeping highly skilled programmers is an ongoing challenge.

Producing programs, and then maintaining them, requires capable programmers. IT managers face cost struggles continuously. In most businesses, IT is a cost center, with a budget. It is a balancing act: keeping programming going in the midst of rising employment costs and a shrinking allocation of money with which to get the job done. Management must either do more with the existing people or let some people go.

To help solve this dilemma, IT management needs its programmers to become more efficient because, in most cases, management really doesn't want to release employees. Becoming more efficient can take many forms, and one way is for the programming staff to stay current on the latest capabilities of the programming language.

## Conclusions

Can free-format RPG IV claim to be more efficient (in other words, more productive) than the fixed-format alternative? I believe the answer is yes—after a short training time. My claim for efficiency is "overall," not in development per se. The majority of increased efficiency comes during the program maintenance phase, where 80 percent of the costs lie.

Consider the programming style attributes described earlier in this chapter: good field naming (including named indicators), indented logic structures, prolific use of comments (on each line if possible), and no Goto operations. If program authors used these techniques, would maintenance programmers be more efficient? I say yes.

# Check It Out

Free-format RPG IV is now fairly well accepted, and it offers us as RPG programmers a significant opportunity to improve the quality and maintainability of our work, to learn modern programming skills, and to stay current in our craft. I encourage you to get to know this "new RPG," and I look forward to the new options yet to come in this form of the language.

# 3

# Free-Format H, F, D, and P Specifications

Technology Refresh 7 (TR7) of the IBM i 7.1 operating system (late 2013) brought major changes to free-format RPG IV. Prior to this event, only RPG's calculation specifications were available in free format.

With these enhancements, the control (H), file (F), definition (D), and procedure (P) specifications are all now free format. This chapter describes those changes, explaining how each compares with its fixed-format equivalent and giving some examples.

One more feature came to RPG IV in TR7: The /Free and /End-free compiler directives are no longer required in our calculations.

## The H (Control) Specification

RPG IV's control specification was almost free-format already, using keywords and values. In the new control specification, you enter information in positions 8 through 80, similar to the requirements we have had in calculations.

Control specifications now begin with a new operation code, Ctl-opt (for control option), followed by the same keyword and value parameters that have long been available to us. At the end of the Ctl-opt statement, you enter a semicolon (;).

You can have multiple Ctl-opt statements, if desired, and you can mix fixed- and free-format statements if needed, due to possible /Copy directives.

An enhancement is that if you specify the Actgrp (activation group), Bnddir (binding directory), or Stgmdl (storage model) keyword, you can omit the Dftactgrp(*No) keyword and value.

Here are two examples:

```
Ctl-opt option(*srcstmt:nodebugio) actgrp(QILE) bnddir('MYBDIR');
```

This control specification tells the compiler to use source statement numbers when reporting compile-time errors, tells the debugger to stop only once on input/output operations, specifies activation group QILE to the program loader, and tells the binder to use binding directory MYBDIR when locating procedures. The Dftactgrp(*No) keyword-value pair is not needed.

```
Ctl-opt bnddir('QC2LE') actgrp(*New);
```

This control specification tells the binder to find C functions in IBM-supplied binding directory QC2LE, and it directs the loader to use activation group *New.

## The F (File) Specifications

Free-format file specifications apply to full procedural files and output files. There is no free-format support for primary/secondary (cycle) files, Record Address (RAF) files, or table files. You can still use these files, but you must use fixed format to specify them. You can mix free- and fixed-format statements now, and without the use of /Free or /End-free directives.

Files are now declared, using a file definition that begins with Dcl-f. After this prefix, you code one or more spaces prior to specifying the file name. File names can be longer than the usual maximum of 10 characters if the Extfile and Extdesc keywords are used. If no device type is specified, the file is assumed to be device Disk.

Here are two examples:

```
Dcl-f MASTER;
```

The statement above defines a database file named MASTER.

```
Dcl-f Last_Years_Sales Extdesc('SALES13') Extfile(textdesc);
```

This example uses keyword Extdesc to specify the file SALES13. Again, the file device defaults to Disk.

For non-database files, you specify the device type after the file name. Here is an example of a printer file:

```
Dcl-f SALESRPT  printer  oflind(overflow);
```

Notice the use of the familiar file keyword Oflind (overflow indicator). Other file keywords that you know and have used are still available.

Another new aspect of free-format files is the Usage keyword. The possibilities are one (or more) of the following values: *Input, *Output, *Update, and *Delete.

Each device type has a default usage value. For disk files, the default is *Input (read only). If you specify *Update on a disk file, *Input will be included as well. If you will be updating and adding new records to the file, you must specify both *Update and *Output. If you will be deleting records in the file, you will need to specify the *Delete usage. This differs from fixed format, where an *Update file included the delete function. Now, you must use the *Delete usage.

For workstation devices, the default usage is both *Input and *Output, so you likely will not have to specify the Usage keyword for this type of device file.

For printer devices, the default usage is *Output, so, again, you probably will not need to specify the Usage keyword for printer files.

For devices Seq and Special, the default usage is *Input.

For disk files, another important keyword is needed routinely: the Keyed keyword. Specify this keyword if you will be using keyed operations, such as SetII or Chain (by key), on the file.

The following examples show how the Usage and Keyed keywords are used in file definitions.

```
Dcl-f  Master Usage(*Delete:*Output) keyed;
```

In this definition, file Master can be accessed for input, update, delete, and output (write) functions. Because keyword Keyed is specified, access to the file will be by the file's key.

```
Dcl-f orders usage(*Output) keyed;
```

Here, the only function available to this file is output (write). The Keyed option requires key fields to be loaded with the correct values before writing the record.

Program-described printer files are still common, so for those of you to whom this applies, here is an example of a program-described printer file in free format:

```
Dcl-f Qprint printer(120);
```

Because this statement specifies the print line length (120), the file Qprint is considered program-described. The actual print lines are described in output specifications.

# The D (Definition) Specifications

As with files, data definitions are now declared (Dcl), followed by a hyphen, followed by the old definition type (e.g., Dcl-s, Dcl-ds, Dcl-pr, Dcl-c).

Following the Dcl-x and one or more spaces is the data name. This name can be long now because there is no longer a need for the ellipsis (...) as there was in fixed format. For extra-long names, you can still use the ellipsis. For data items that do not need a name, specify *N as the name.

New to this free-format style is the addition of End statements for data structures (End-ds), prototypes (End-pr), and procedure interfaces (End-pi). You can optionally enter the data name between the End-xx and the semicolon.

In a data structure, if the subfield name happens to have the same name as an operation code (e.g., Select), then a prefix, Dcl-Subf, is needed before the subfield name. For example:

```
Dcl-Subf Select;
```

Another new aspect to the free-format data definitions is the use of data type keywords with values for some. Table 3-1 lists the data types followed by the keyword/values to be used in declaring the data item.

| Table 3-1: Data types for free-format data definitions | |
|---|---|
| **String data types:** | |
| Fixed-length character | char(*characters*) |
| Fixed-length graphic | graph(*characters*) |
| Fixed-length UCS2 | UCS2(*characters*) |
| Varying-length character | VarChar(*characters*) |
| Varying-length graphic | VarGraph(*characters*) |
| Varying-length UCS2 | VarUCS2(*characters*) |
| Varying-length with specific prefix size:<br>        Character<br>        Graphic<br>        UCS2 | <br>VarChar(*characters*:4)<br>VarGraph(*characters*:4)<br>VarUCS2(*characters*:4) |
| **Numeric data types:** | |
| Decimal with zero decimal positions | packed(*digits*)<br>zoned(*digits*)<br>BinDec(*digits*) |
| Decimal with decimal positions | packed(*digits:decimals*)<br>zoned(*digits:decimals*)<br>BinDec(*digits:decimals*) |
| Integer | Int(*digits*)<br>3, 5, 10, 20 |
| Unsigned integer | Uns(*digits*)<br>3, 5, 10, 20 |
| Float | Float(*bytes*)<br>4, 8                          *Continued* |
| *Note: The BinDec type is similar to the old B (binary) data type. It refers to a decimal number stored in binary form, but not a true binary number.* | |

| Table 3-1: Data types for free-format data definitions (continued) | |
|---|---|
| **Other data types:** | |
| Indicator | Ind |
| Pointer | Pointer |
| Procedure pointer | Pointer(*Proc) |
| Date | Date |
| Date with format | Date(*YMD-) |
| Time | Time |
| Time with format | Time(*HMS-) |
| Timestamp | Timestamp |
| Object | Object(*Java:*class*) |

Here are a few examples of declaring data items.

```
Dcl-c Twenty 20;
```

This first statement defines a named constant, Twenty, with value 20.

```
Dcl-s Total packed(11:2);
```

This one defines a variable named Total that is data type packed decimal, with length 11 digits and 2 decimal positions.

```
Dcl-s First_Err ind;
```

This statement defines the named indicator First_Err.

```
Dcl-s  i  uns(5);
```

This declaration line defines variable i as an unsigned integer with values from 0 to around 64k. This variable will likely be used as an index for arrays or data structures.

A new keyword is now available for use in data structures. The Pos (position) keyword is used as a replacement for "from" and "to" numbers and the Overlay keyword.

Here are two examples:

```
Dcl-ds  Indicators;
    Exit          Ind    Pos(3);
    Cancel        Ind    Pos(12);
    Page_down     Ind    Pos(25);
End-ds;
```

The indicator data structure declared above uses the Pos keyword instead of from and to numbers.

```
Dcl-ds  *N   PSDS;  // The *N means no name
    PgmName   Char(10)    Pos(1);
    Status    Zoned(5:0)  Pos(11);
    User      Char(10)    Pos(254);
End-ds;
```

This example demonstrates the use of the program status data structure. The name is specified as *N, and the keyword PSDS is used to denote this. The code uses the Pos keyword instead of from and to numbers.

Next are some examples of prototypes and procedure interface definitions.

```
Dcl-Pr  EX05R  Extpgm;
    *N      packed(2:0);
    *N      packed(7:0);
End-Pr;

Dcl-Pi  EX05R;
    Company_No   packed(2:0);
    Customer_No  packed(7:0);
End-Pi;
```

The prototype above defines a dynamic call and would be used in the calling program, with the procedure interface below it in the called program.

```
Dcl-Pr  EX10  End-Pr;
```

This is an example of declaring a prototype for calling external program EX10 where there are no parameters. Notice that the End-pr can be placed on the same line as the declaration.

# The P (Procedure) Specification

As with files and definitions, our subprocedures are now declared. The suffix after Dcl- is Proc, so the syntax is very simple. Here is an example:

```
Dcl-proc  Addparms;
   Dcl-pi *N    packed(9:2);
       Addp1  packed(5:2);
       Addp2  packed(5:2);
   End-pi;
Return  Addp1 + Addp2;
End-proc;
```

The Dcl-proc line is similar to the first fixed-format P specification that begins a subprocedure. The Dcl-pi is a replacement for the old D spec with PI. Because the procedure interface shares the same name as the Dcl-proc, the *N may be used. Otherwise, only the procedure name can be used. The two parameters are next, using the new packed data type naming. The procedure interface ends with End-pi. The procedure action, done on the Return statement, is adding the two parameters with the sum as the return value. The End-proc statement ends the subprocedure.

It is becoming common practice to put subprocedures in a no-main module, put this module in a service program, and make these subprocedures available to be bound. To do this, specify the Export keyword on the procedure definition.

To make the previous example available for binding, the first line would be as follows:

```
Dcl-proc   Addparms  export;
```

Also remember that no /Free or /End-free directives are needed in your procedural statements.

# Conclusions

The new free-format options for H, F, D, and P specifications will have a profound effect on RPG IV programming. We have been given some new ways to code our RPG programs, in a format that is truly contemporary, similar to the other languages of our day.

# 4

# Introducing
# Free-Format RPG IV

The ability to create free-format calculations in RPG IV became available with the arrival of Version 5 Release 1 of WebSphere® Development Studio, IBM's application development tool suite for the IBM i operating system. Free format's arrival caused little fanfare back then, and most RPG IV developers with whom I spoke at the time weren't very interested in the concept.

Early on, some of my RPG IV programmer friends tried to use free format and asked me for help in their work. The ambitious ones who gave it a try found themselves pleased with the results. However, due to limitations in the first release of free format, RPG calculations still required many lines of fixed-format code, such as for Klist and Kfld operations. Mixing fixed- and free-format calculations made programs look "clunky" and certainly didn't help convince co-workers to convert to the new style.

In V5R2, IBM provided additional functionality that let RPG IV programmers use key arguments within a free-format Chain or Setxx operation or use the %Kds built-in function with a data structure. These enhancements represented a big step forward in "de-clunking" the calculations. Other new functions, such as the += accumulative assignment operator (which adds the result of an expression to the target of the assignment), gave free-format RPG procedures a C- and Java-like appearance. Additional built-in functions at that time also helped to modernize RPG IV's procedures.

Today, free-format calculations in RPG IV can look like any other modern programming language. Newcomers to RPG IV programming who have prior experience in C, Cobol, PL/1, or another free-format language find free-format RPG IV simple to learn and use. Now that free-format calculations have gained a modicum of acceptance, many fixed-format RPG IV "old-timers" are taking a good look at the free-format style.

For those new to free format, getting started is sometimes the toughest part. Frankly, it's not easy to change the way you've done something for a long time, especially programming. If you have come this far and want to try writing a little program in the new format, this book will help you begin. We start our tour of free-format calculations in this chapter, with an overview of the free-format structure and a look at some key operations and features.

## Coding Free-Format Calculations

The first step in writing free-format calculations is remembering to place your free-format RPG IV code in position 8 or beyond. Positions 1–5 are available for anything (e.g., change control information). Position 6 must be remain blank, and position 7 is reserved for compiler directives, such as /SQL. Free-format calculations end in position 80.

All supported free-format operations, as well as all built-in functions, are available to you. In contrast to its fixed-format older brother, which has 153 operations, free-format RPG IV provides just 62 free-format operations (as of V7.1). However, free-format RPG IV isn't simply a "stripped-down" subset of its fixed-format counterpart. IBM has created many built-in functions to provide functionality equivalent to (or better than) most of the "missing" operation codes. As of V7.1, RPG IV provides a total of 80 built-in functions.

A line of free-format source begins with a free-format operation code, followed by one or more spaces, the Factor 1 operand, one or more additional spaces, and then the Factor 2 operand. Free-format RPG IV has no result field operand. Instead, you perform arithmetic and character-management operations using assignment statements (Eval operations without the Eval).

An implication of no result field is the inability to define work variables "on the fly" as RPG programmers commonly did years ago. However, thanks to the powerful nature of free-format expressions, we don't need as many work fields

today, and declaring them in definition specifications makes program maintenance easier and more productive.

The final requirement for a line of free-format RPG IV source is a termin-
ating semicolon (;), followed by a comment if desired. You enter a comment by
keying two slashes (//) followed by the text of the comment. You can also place
comments on a line by themselves.

Listing 4-1 shows a sample block of free-format code, including a few free-
format operations and some comments.

```
Miles_per_gallon = Miles / Gallons;
Eval(h) Pay = Hourly_rate * Hours;
       // An entire line comment
Name = %trim(First_n) + ' ' + %trim(Last_n);
Error_cust_no = *On;    // Short comment on a calculation line
```

*Listing 4-1: Sample free-format block*

## *Naming Variables*

Free-format RPG IV's rules for naming variables are no different from fixed
format's, but when employing longer names (more than 14 characters), you
must use either the extended Factor 2 format or free format in your calculations.
Variable names must begin with a character and can be in any case. The character can be any one of the 26 regular alphabet characters or the special character #,
$, @, or _. Numbers (0-9) are optional and can be used after the first character.
Variable names cannot contain blanks, but you can use the underscore character
(_) as a word separator to form a multiword name (e.g., Miles_per_gallon).

Until RPG IV came along in late 1994, RPG variable names were limited
to six characters. This limitation included references to arrays and their indexes.
The first version of RPG IV supported 10-character names, matching the size
maximum in DDS for variable naming. A few years ago, IBM extended the
variable-name length to its present limit of 4,096! Not many programmers are
interested in using such long names, but it's sure nice not to be constrained
either.

Free-format RPG has a "semi" restriction for variable naming. In free format,
the Eval operation code may be dropped if no op-code extenders are needed.
However, if a variable name uses the same spelling as an operation code—such
as In, Out, Select, and others—you must specify the Eval operation code when the
variable is used on the left side of the assignment. I suggest not using variables

that are named the same as operation codes, to eliminate confusion and restrictions.

## Programming Style

No other rules apply when entering source statements in free-format calculations. However, good programming style should prompt us to enter statements in an ordered way that makes a program's logic easier to understand during program maintenance. Good style would dictate entering a program's "outer" logic as far left as possible (position 8) and beginning "inner" logic two spaces to the right. Continue this indenting process until you're about halfway across the page. If you need deeper groups, you will have to decide whether to continue to the right or to start over again at position 8.

Listing 4-2 shows a free-format code block that uses indenting to make the program logic more apparent.

```
Dou %eof;
  ReadC SubfileRec;
  If not %eof;
    Fielda = Fieldb;
    If Fieldc <> *zero;
      Error_Msg_1 = *On;
      RI_Fieldc = *On;
      Sflnxtchg = *On;
    Endif;
    Update SubfileRec;
  Endif;
  ReadC SubfileRec;
Enddo;
```

Listing 4-2: Example of indenting free-format calculations

## A Note About Case

RPG IV has no rules regarding the case of variables, operation codes, and comments in source statements, but some programmers suggest using a style that capitalizes each "word" in variables and uses lower case otherwise (for example, SubfileRec). Others recommend fully capitalizing all externally defined variables. The compiler translates all variables and operation codes (other than character strings within apostrophes) to upper case before analyzing the code, so whatever case options you choose are purely a personal decision.

# Free-Format Operation Codes

Table 4-1 lists the 62 operations that free-format RPG IV supports as of V7.1.
Appendix A describes each of these operations in detail. All built-in functions
are also available to you in free format. Many built-in functions, such as %Check,
%Lookup, and %Scan, provide operation code functionality. Some, such as
%Check, provide exactly the same function as an operation code, while others,
such as %Lookup, provide additional capabilities.

| Table 4-1: Free-format operations | |
|---|---|
| **Operation** | **Description** |
| Acq | Acquire a program device (used in ICF files). |
| Begsr | Begin a subroutine. |
| CallP | Call a prototyped procedure (you can also call procedures implicitly, omitting the CallP). |
| Chain | Access a record from a file directly by key or relative record number. |
| Clear | Set all items in a data structure, record format, array, or variable to zero or blank, depending on the data type. |
| Close | Close a file that has been opened using the Open operation. |
| Commit | Commit file changes made since the last Commit or Rolbk operation. |
| Dealloc | Deallocate dynamic storage. |
| Delete | Delete a record from a file. |
| Dou | Do until (a logical group ending with Enddo). |
| Dow | Do while (a logical group ending with Enddo). |
| Dsply | Display a message. |
| Dump | Dump a program (variables, record contents, and so on). |
| Else | Else (part of an If group). |
| Elseif | Else and If combined (part of an If group). |
| Endxx | End a group of logic or monitor operations; the suffix xx must match the starting operation (i.e., Enddo, Endfor, Endif, EndMon, or Endsl). |
| Endsr | End of subroutine. |
| Eval | Evaluate an assignment expression; if a character string is specified, the result is left-justified (assignment is possible without explicitly specifying the Eval operation code). |
| EvalR | Evaluate an assignment expression; character strings are right-justified. |
| Eval-Corr | Assign corresponding subfields in data structures. *Continued* |

| Table 4-1: Free-format operations (continued) | |
|---|---|
| Except | Perform exception output (program-described on output specifications). |
| Exfmt | Write and then read a record format (often called "Execute a format"). |
| Exsr | Perform a subroutine (often called "Execute a subroutine"). |
| Feod | Force end of data. |
| For | Begin a logic group, ending in Endfor, that uses a specified index and counts up or down to a specified limit. |
| Force | Force a specified file to be read next (used only if the cycle is desired). |
| If | Begin a logic group, ending in Endif, that may have Else or Elseif inside the logic group. |
| In | Retrieve data from a data area and load the named data structure. |
| Iter | Iterate, or jump to the most current Enddo or Endfor. |
| Leave | Leave, or jump out of the most current Do or For group to the next statement after the Enddo or EndFor. |
| LeaveSR | Leave a subroutine. |
| Monitor | Begin a monitor group, ending with an EndMon, to handle error situations in a section of code. |
| Next | Force the next input to come from the specified program device. |
| On-Error | Used in a Monitor group to specify an error condition and begin handling if true. |
| Open | Open a file that was specified as user open on the file declaration. |
| Other | Used in a Select/When group to handle the condition "none of the above." |
| Out | Write the contents of the named data structure to a data area. |
| Post | Update the file information data structure for the named program device or file. |
| Read | Read next (forward in the file); the operand can be a record name or file name. |
| ReadC | Read a changed record (used only for subfiles within a display file). |
| ReadE | Read equal—A multifunction operation that compares a specified operand with the current file index, and if the operand matches the current key, reads a record. If they are not equal, eof is set. |
| ReadP | Read prior (backward in the file); the operand can be a record name or file name. |
| ReadPE | Read prior equal (the same as ReadE, but reading backward). |
| Rel | Release a program device. |
| Reset | Reset a data item to its initialized value. |

| | |
|---|---|
| Return | Return—Used in two contexts: at the end of a subprocedure with an optional expression or elsewhere to return to the caller of the procedure. |
| RolBk | Roll back—Used with commitment control to remove file changes made since the last Commit or RolBk operation. |
| Select | Begin a logic group requiring When statements and ending with Endsl. |
| Setgt | Set file pointer greater than (a parameter is used to set the file pointer to the record whose key value is closest to but greater than the parameter). |
| Setll | Set file pointer greater than or equal (used to be called "lower limit," thus the LL. The file pointer is set to the record whose key is equal to or greater than the specified parameter). |
| SortA | Sort an array (the array to sort is specified as a parameter; the order is specified on the array definition). |
| Test | Test a date, time, or timestamp for validity, or test a character or numeric field for a valid date or time. |
| Unlock | Unlock a data area object, or release a record lock. |
| Update | Update a record previously read via a Read or Chain operation. |
| When | Part of a Select group used to specify a condition to test, similar to If. |
| Write | Write a new record to a file. |
| XML-Into | Parse an XML document into a variable. |
| XML-Sax | SAX Parse for an XML document. |

Perhaps more interesting than which operations are present in free format is which fixed-format operations are not included in the set of free-format operations. Some frequently used fixed-format operations didn't make the cut. Table 4-2 lists a sampling.

| Table 4-2: Examples of fixed-format–only operation codes | |
|---|---|
| Add | Move |
| Call (Dynamic call) | Movea |
| CallB (Bound call) | Mult |
| CASxx (Case) | Mvr |
| Cat | Scan |
| Div | Setoff |
| Do | Seton |
| End | Sub |
| Goto | Subst |
| Lookup | Tag |

Most of these operation codes have a free-format counterpart to which you can easily convert. The Seton and Setoff operations, for example, have been replaced by the Eval operation (as in Eval *In21= *On). Another example, Mvr, is easily converted to the %Rem built-in function. And you can replace a Lookup operation with one of five %Lookup or five %Tlookup built-in functions, depending on whether you are searching an array or a table.

It would be nice if all the unsupported operations from fixed format had a simple equivalent in free format, but this is not the case. Some fixed-format operations, such as Move, have no clean and easy conversion path to free format. In Chapter 11, I provide solutions for some of the tough ones (of which, fortunately, there are few). Perhaps one day IBM will provide additional built-in functions or other methods to address the more difficult conversion situations.

In the rest of this section, I describe some of free-format RPG IV's more commonly used operations (as well as built-in functions where needed) and show some examples to illustrate their use. If you are already writing calculations using the extended Factor 2 format rather than RPG's original fixed format, you will find much of this material familiar.

## Evaluate

The most common operation in free-format RPG IV doesn't even use an operation code. It's the evaluate (Eval) operation, minus the Eval operation code. This form of evaluate is usually called an *assignment statement*. The evaluate operation evaluates the expression specified to the right of the equal sign (=) and assigns the result to the receiving item on the left side of the equal sign. The receiving side is cleared for the default length of the item or for the specified length if substringing is used. This is the way other free-format languages work, too. In fact, CL's CHGVAR (Change Variable) command functions this way for its VAR parameter.

When performing mathematical calculations, you sometimes want the result rounded (half adjusted). The assignment statement doesn't perform this rounding, but you can accomplish it by entering the Eval operation code to the left of the assignment statement and specifying the half-adjust operation extender, h. You specify other operation extenders, such as precision (r), in the same way.

Listing 4-3 shows several examples of assignment statements.

```
Dcl-S Field30 Char(30);
Dcl-S Field10 Char(10) Inz('ABCDEFGHIJ');
Dcl-S Field3 Char(3);

Field30 = Field10;      // Field30 is cleared, and then Field10 is
                        // moved to it, left-justified

Eval(h) Pay = Hourly_rate * hours;  // The math is performed (with
                        // rounding) and the result assigned to Pay


          // More complex forms

*In03 = F7 = F3;        // This statement checks to see whether F7
                        // is equal to F3. If yes, *In03 is set to
                        // *On, but if F7 is not equal to F3, *In03
                        // is set to *Off

*In21 = *In43 or (Pay > 100);  // This statement sets *In21 to *On
                        // if either *In43 is *On or Pay > 100

%subst(Field30:5:4) = 'xyz';   // Positions 5-8 of Field30 are
                        // cleared, then 'xyz' is moved to 5-7

Field3 = *In03 + (Pay > 100) + %eof(FileA);  // Three items are
                        // evaluated as true or false and then
                        // concatenated, with the result of Field3
                        // equal to '000', '001', '010', and so on
```

*Listing 4-3: Sample assignment statements*

# If

Another popular operation code, supported both in fixed and free format, is the If operation, along with its associated operations Else, Elseif, and Endif. The free-format version of If is similar to the extended Factor 2 method, but it gives you the added freedom of being able to place the specifications anywhere within the line (or lines). Parentheses, in addition to the logical operators And and Or, provide a significant improvement in programming ease over the previous Ifxx operation.

Many people are not aware that RPG had no If at all until RPG III (circa 1979). IBM retrofitted the operation into RPG II around 1990. In case you're wondering how programmers performed "If" logic in RPG before If was invented, the operation used (and still supported today) was Comp (Compare), along with lots of indicators.

The Elseif operation is a relative newcomer to RPG IV, new with V5R1. Its use can simplify a long set of nested Ifs and Elses. Elseif is equivalent to an Else operation followed immediately by an If. You need only one Endif at the end of an If/Elseif group, regardless of how many Elseifs the group contains. One set of statements may be performed in the If and Elseif blocks of code, or possibly none. This functionality follows the same scheme as the Select and When operations (you'll learn more about those two operations in Chapter 6).

Interestingly, you can't shorten the Endif operation to End in free format. In fact, free format doesn't support the End operation at all. Correct "Ends" force us as programmers to put the appropriate "End*xx*" at the end of a set of logic. It's a small thing, but program clarity is improved.

Listing 4-4 illustrates the use of If, Else, Elseif, and Endif operations in free format.

```
If  A = B;                   // Simple If, Else, and Endif
   FieldA = FieldB;
Else;
   FieldA = *Zero;
Endif;


        // An If, Elseif, Else, and Endif group
If Option = 'A' and (Type = 3 or Company = 73);
   Value = 1;
Elseif Option = 'B' and (Type = 3 or Company = 75);
   Value = 2;
Elseif Option = 'C' and (Type = 1 or Company = 99);
   Value = 3;
Else;
   Value = 4;
Endif;
```

Listing 4-4: Examples of If, Elseif, Else, and Endif

## *Controlled Looping*

Controlled looping is another common function in RPG, and IBM made some changes for free format in RPG IV. The most important change is the absence of Goto. To use or not to use a Goto operation (in any programming language) is a topic that programmers have hotly debated. But in free-format RPG IV, there is no debate; Goto simply is not there. To accomplish controlled looping, you use Dou (Do until), Dow (Do while), and For (For) groups.

Doing without Goto can improve the readability and performance of your programs. Knowing that you can't use Goto forces you to consider other options.

We are still free to code using our personal preferences, but eliminating Goto removes one of the biggest issues in RPG: spaghetti code. For those unfamiliar with the term, "spaghetti code" is code that jumps around in a program using Goto and Tag operations without regard to program structure. Spaghetti code is thus very difficult to maintain. RPG isn't uniquely vulnerable to spaghetti code; any language that provides a Goto function is at risk. With free-format RPG IV, this issue is behind us.

You may have noticed that another popular looping operation, Do, is missing in free-format RPG IV. This operation is easily converted to the superior For operation, which provides both indexing up to a limit and indexing down from a high starting value to a bottom limit.

Listing 4-5 shows examples of controlled looping in RPG IV. We will discuss the looping operations used in the examples, along with other operations for controlling program flow, in greater detail in Chapter 6.

```
For i = 1 to 20;                  // Loop setup - perform 20 times
  If NewArray(i) = *zero;         // Using the loop index i
    NewArray(i) = OldArray(i);
  Endif;
Endfor;

For i = %len(LName) downto 3;  // High to low loop
  If %subst(LName:i-2:3) = 'Jr.';     // Using the index in
                                      // a substring
    Suffix = 'Junior';
    Leave;                            // Leave the For loop
  Endif;
Endfor;
```

*Continued*

```
    Read FileA;
    Dow not %eof(FileA);                // Do While loop
      // Process record...
      Read FileA;
    Enddo;

    Dou exit;                           // Do Until loop
      Exfmt RecA;
      If not exit;
        Select;
          When Exit;
          When Pagedown;
            Exsr Loadpage;
          Other;
            Exsr Edit;
        Endsl;
      Endif;
    Enddo;
```

Listing 4-5: Controlled looping examples

## Mathematics

You code mathematical expressions in free format using the same methods as fixed format's extended Factor 2. The standard math functions of add, subtract, multiply, and divide are performed within expressions using the +, -, *, and / operators, respectively. IBM also introduced the exponentiation operator (**) in RPG IV, permitting an expression to use a fraction, whole number, or mixed number as an exponent. This operator adds a powerful capability to the language that was previously unavailable without calling a C program. The free-format option gives you more room on a line for complex mathematical expressions.

## Character Strings

You construct character-string expressions in free format just as you do for fixed format's extended Factor 2. Many built-in functions pertain to character strings or converting numeric information to character.

# Programming Style Issues

Many books and articles have covered the subject of programming with style. RPG hasn't played much of a role in style discussions, due mainly to the fixed-format nature of its calculations. Now, with free format, RPG programmers can, and should, pay attention to matters of style. With that goal in mind, here are some points to remember as you get started coding in free-format RPG IV.

## *Mixing Formats*

Today's RPG IV language is flexible enough to let you code in any of three basic formats that I will call original, extended Factor 2, and free format. The original format (still available) includes support for level break, one condition indicator, Factor 1, Operation code, Factor 2, Result, Result definition, and three resulting indicator areas. Many fixed-format operations require this format. It requires a C in position 6, and line comments (denoted by *) start in position 7.

Extended Factor 2 came into being with the advent of RPG IV, and IBM has enhanced it over the years. It is really a semi–free-format option that has gained a wide margin of acceptance. This format still has level break and conditional indicator capability, although programmers seldom use these options today. The operation codes that exploit the extended Factor 2 format are limited to CallP, Dou, Dow, Eval, For, If/Elseif, Return (in a subprocedure), and Select/When. Extended Factor 2 operations still require a C in position 6, comments (*) starting in position 7, and Factor 1 in positions 13–26. This format mixes easily with RPG's original fixed format.

You can combine fixed-format (both original and extended Factor 2) and free-format calculations within the same program, but the resulting code, although perfectly functional, may not look very good or be maintained easily by other programmers. Listing 4-6 shows a program segment that mixes use of RPG's original format, the extended Factor 2 format, and free format in its calculations. As you can see, the result is a jumble of various types of source code that will take a maintenance programmer a while to make sense of.

```
C* Original
C        CustKey       Klist
C                      Kfld                    Customer#
C                      Kfld                    Cust_Code
C        CustKey       Chain    CustFile
C* Extended Factor 2
C                      If       %found(CustFile)
C* Original
C        TotSales      Add      Sales          TotSales

         // Now handle more sales processing
      Setll (Customer#) SalesFile;   // Sales record check
      If %equal;                     // Not a new customer
        Chain Customer# SalesFile;   // Get sales record
      Else;
        Exsr Add_Sales_Rec;          // Need to add customer to sales file
      Endif;
      Exsr Sales_Routine;            // Process sales for this customer

C* Original
C                      Endif
C        TotSales      Lookup   Array(i)                        99  99
C        *In99         Ifeq     *On
C        Array(i)      Add      TotSales       Array(i)
C*
C* Further processing, etc.
C*
```

*Listing 4-6: Examples of mixing the original format, extended Factor 2, and free format*

Now take a look at Listing 4-7. This version of the code shows how writing all your calculations in free format can improve the readability of your programs. The flow of control is clear, ample comments explain each key operation, and the code will be easier for another programmer to understand and modify when the need arises to do so.

```
Chain (Customer#:Cust_Code) CustFile;  // Checking cust. record
If %found(CustFile);                   // All OK
  TotSales += Sales;                   // Accumulate sales
  Setll (Customer#) SalesFile;         // Sales record check
  If %equal;                           // Not a new customer
    Chain Customer# SalesFile;         // Get sales record
  Else;
    Exsr Add_Sales_Rec;                // Add customer to sales file
  Endif;
  Exsr Sales_Routine;                  // Process sales for this customer
Endif;
i = %lookupge(TotSales:Array:1);
If i > *zero;
  Array(i) += TotSales;
Endif;
  // Further processing
```

*Listing 4-7: Sample calculations using free format only*

As you update old programs and write free-format code to your level of comfort, it is likely you will have some programs that mix fixed and free format. When considering free format, though, you must eventually decide whether to continue mixing formats or to adopt free format for all your calculations. I believe that the authors of the free-format RPG IV compiler anticipated this decision point and provided ample functionality entirely in free format. In effect, they wrote a compiler within a compiler. They could have separated the free-format capability from the other formats and come up with an entirely new language, but they didn't—at least so far.

While we are on the subject of the "old" and the "new," let me note that companies that are still converting their RPG/400 programs to RPG IV using IBM's CVTRPGSRC (Convert RPG Source) command do not have an option for free format. However, a third-party vendor, Linoma Software, includes a free-format option in its program-conversion offerings. IBM's Rational® Developer for i (RDi) software has a conversion utility that converts RPG/400 to free-format RPG IV. Neither of the conversion programs provides a complete conversion. There are several fixed-format operations that do not convert easily, so converted programs may have a mixture of fixed and free-format statements.

## Keyed Access

Keeping your code totally free of any fixed-format calculations brings some other coding factors into play. Without Klist and Kfld operations, for example, you must use either a data structure (with the *Key option) and the %Kds built-in function (for Chain and Setxx operations) or in-line key arguments. I prefer to use in-line arguments when there are only a few arguments but use the %Kds function grudgingly when there are many arguments. That's because with the %Kds method, you need to load the data structure subfields before using Chain or Setxx, but with the in-line method no additional lines are needed.

Listing 4-8 illustrates each of these methods. (For the inline example, assume the same file (FileA) and record (RecA) as used in the data structure example.)

---

**First, the key data structure method—**

*Data file DDS for FileA:*
```
     A             R RecA
     A               Field1          20A
     A               Field2           9S 2
     A               Field3          30A
     A             K Field1
     A             K Field2
```

*RPG IV program:*
```
     Dcl-F FileA keyed;

     Dcl-DS KeyRec LikeRec(RecA:*key);
     End-DS;
         //    KeyRec is a qualified data structure

     // First, load the key search arguments
     KeyRec.Field1 = data1;
     KeyRec.Field2 = data2;
     // Now we can use the data structure as the key search argument
     Chain %kds(KeyRec) FileA;
```

**Now, the in-line way—**
```
     // Just use the runtime data variables
     Chain (Data1:Data2) FileA;
```

---

*Listing 4-8: Using the key data structure method and in-line key list parameters*

## Named Indicators

The ability to name an indicator came to RPG IV around V5R1 without much ado. I saw this enhancement as a great leap forward in the modernization of the RPG language. The indicator data type puts RPG on par with other modern languages that feature similar data types, such as C, Cobol, Java, and even CL. RPG IV's indicator data type is equivalent to a variable defined in CL as *LGL (logical). Other languages call this primitive a Boolean, meaning that 0 (zero) and 1 (one) are its only permitted values. RPG IV's named indicators have all the same attributes as the numbered ones, except that they can't be used in fixed-format operations that set a resulting indicator.

Named indicators can add value to your programs, but only if you name them well. Naming an indicator Flag22 is no better than using a numbered indicator, but a name such as Invalid_acct_num can make your program easier to read and maintain.

## Naming File Indicators

In addition to naming "general-purpose" indicators, you can name the indicators associated with a file, especially a display file. Using good names for conditioning or response indicators is sometimes difficult. Keep reminding yourself that longer names are okay.

To name a file indicator, first specify the file-level keyword INDARA in the file's DDS. Doing so causes a separate indicator area to be generated for the file. (Our friends coding in Cobol have used this technique for a long time, but we in RPG haven't needed it.) Then, in the RPG IV program, specify keyword INDDS (indicator data structure) on the file declaration, providing the name of a data structure as the keyword value.

Next, code the named data structure in in the data structure declaration. Each subfield entry matches an indicator used in the file. Here is where you specify the name of the indicator. For internal type, enter an n and either "from" and "to" numbers matching the indicator number or, in the keyword area, keyword Overlay(*parm1:parm2*), where *parm1* is the data structure name and *parm2* is the indicator number. If you "double-use" indicators (in different formats), simply make up another subfield using a different name and the same indicator number. Just be sure you're careful in this practice.

One more thing. When using the indicator data structure, the RPG program no longer knows the file indicators by their numbers, only by their names. The numbered indicators are no longer used for the file.

Another indicator-related change that IBM made to RPG IV is the ability to name the overflow indicator used on printer files. Specify a defined named indicator on the OFLIND (Overflow indicator) keyword of the printer file's file description. This named indicator is set on automatically when a print line is on or after the specified overflow line. The named indicator must be set off after overflow processing to avoid invalid overflow processing.

Note that there is one situation in which you must continue to use a two-letter indicator: You must still use the LR indicator to terminate a program.

Listing 4-9 shows examples of naming indicators.

```
       // Named indicators
       Dcl-S First_Time Ind;
       Dcl-S Invalid_Cust Ind;


DDS in a display file named DSPFile:

 A                                          INDARA
 A                                          CA03(03)
   * Record information...


RPG program:

       Dcl-F DSPFile Workstn Idds(Inds);

       Dcl-DS Inds;
          Exit    Ind Pos(3);
          Cancel  Ind Pos(12);
          SflDsp  Ind Pos(30);
          // Other display file indicators
       End-DS;

       If not exit;       // Using the display file indicator 03 as a name
         Sfldsp = *on;    // Setting a display file indicator
         // More program content here
       Endif;
```

*Listing 4-9: Examples of named indicators and using an indicator data structure*

# Summing Up

Free-format RPG IV is no longer new; however, IBM has enhanced the language with every release since it became available in 2001. Free-format RPG coding is quite different from the original RPG calculation specifications, but it is not too dissimilar to the extended Factor 2 style of coding. Free format's coding rules are easy to remember: operation code, then Factor 1, then Factor 2. Ending a statement with a semicolon is probably the thing you're most likely to forget.

When you code in free format, you will find built-in functions essential. Many operation codes of the fixed-format variety are available only as built-in functions in free-format RPG IV.

With free format, you are free to code lines any which way you like, and the compiler won't care. You'll find that coding free format with style makes all the difference in the world. Other free-form languages (such as C, Java, Pascal, and PL/1) have crossed this figurative "bridge" already, and we can learn from their style. To make our programs better in free format, we must decide to follow style guidelines, such as indenting. We must also use comments—liberally. The addition of named indicators gives free-format RPG IV programmers the ability to code RPG IV like other modern programming languages.

You can still code RPG IV using the original calculation format, nearly the same way the language was coded in the 1960s. Or, you can decide to try this new, free-format approach using some of the style methods suggested in this book. In the next several chapters, I show you how to code common programming requirements in free-format RPG IV. Then we'll examine some special conversion situations and look at four sample programs that illustrate the new RPG IV free-format style of coding.

# 5

# Input/Output
# Using Free Format

Most input and output functions are the same in free-format RPG IV as in fixed format, except for the location of the code within the source line. Another difference is the use of alternatives for a key list used in database I/O for Chain, Set, and similar operations. The key list is replaced by an inline composite argument list or a key data structure and the %Kds built-in function on the I/O operation. Also, database update now features the %Fields built-in function option.

In this chapter, we look at the operations, options, and built-in functions now available for database I/O, as well as for workstation I/O and printer output. You will find that the free-format approach to input and output varies little from the extended Factor 2 calculation format.

## Database Input

Input from database files comes from various operations: Read (Read next), ReadE (Read next equal), ReadP (Read prior), ReadPE (Read prior equal), Chain (Chain), Setll (Set lower limit), and Setgt (Set greater than). The set file pointer operations Setll and Setgt don't provide data from a record, but they can furnish information about a file's key (found or equal) without accessing the record data. Of course, the two set operations also set the file pointer.

If successful, all the read operations and Chain provide data from an entire record. If unsuccessful, these operations set a condition: "end-of-file" for the read operations or "not found" for Chain. In most programs, we check these conditions to determine what to do next. If end-of-file or not found is determined, the record data remains unchanged from a prior successful operation. If no prior successful operation occurred, the fields of the record retain their initial values.

If you are already familiar with the database input operations from your experience with fixed-format RPG, you will have no problem adjusting to free format. The big difference is that we cannot call on resulting indicators in free format, so we must use built-in functions to determine the outcome of attempted input or output functions. The built-in functions—%Eof, %Equal, %Error, and %Found—have been available for extended Factor 2 calculations for several years.

## %Eof

The %Eof built-in function tests a specified file for end-of-file. If you specify no file, %Eof checks the last file read for end-of-file. The function returns a value of the indicator data type: either '1' to signify that the end-of-file condition was met or '0' otherwise.

You can use the %Eof built-in with all read operations. In the case of read prior operations, %Eof lets you test for beginning-of-file. Listing 5-1 shows examples of read operations used with the %Eof built-in function.

```
Read File_A;              // Read first record
Dow not %eof(File_A);     // While not at end-of-file
  // Process record
  Read File_A;            // Read next record
Enddo;

Setgt *Hival File_B;      // Set file pointer to eof
ReadP File_B;             // Read prior - first
Dow not %eof(File_B);     // While not at beg-of-file
  // Process record
  ReadP File_B;           // Read next prior
Enddo;
```

*Listing 5-1: Read operations using the %Eof built-in function*

# %Found

Another built-in function used with database input is %Found. You employ this function after a Chain operation to determine whether the record access was successful. Like the %Eof built-in function, %Found returns a value of the indicator data type: value '1' for record found or '0' for no record found. You can optionally specify the name of the file you want to test with %Found. If you specify no file name, the operation checks the most recent operation that sets a %Found condition. In addition to Chain, the following operations can set %Found: Check, Checkr, Delete, Lookup, Scan, Setgt, and Setll.

In Chapter 4, we reviewed keyed access for Chain and Set operations. Two alternatives are now available that eliminate the need for the Klist (Define a composite key) and Kfld (Define parts of a key) operations.

In the first method, a named data structure defined in definition specifications uses the keyword LikeRec with a data-file record name as its first parameter and the value *Key as its second parameter. (You can also use the keyword ExtName with the data-file record name and *Key.) The record name you specify should match the record name of the file that will be used in the Chain or similar operation in the calculations. The data structure becomes a *qualified* data structure, with subfields referenced using the form *recordname.fieldname*. The subfields of this data structure that are related to the keys of the file will be used as the argument key fields. In the calculations, the %Kds built-in function is used on the Chain, Set, or similar operation. This function has two parameters: the named data structure mentioned above and an optional constant that specifies how many key fields to use from the data structure in the operation. If omitted, the second parameter defaults to all key fields.

The second method available is the inline composite argument list, provided on the calculation operation line. You specify fields in a parameter-style list, and, together, these fields comprise the lookup key argument.

When you use either of these methods, no fixed-format calculations (for Klist and Kfld) are necessary. Listing 5-2 shows sample Chain operations that use the %Found built-in function and the two key list alternatives.

You can also use the %Found built-in function after a Setll or Setgt operation. In this situation, %Found returns the value '1' if there is a key in the file whose value is equal to or greater than the key list argument (for Setll) or whose value is greater than the key list argument (for Setgt).

```
Dcl-DS Rec_Key LikeRec(File_C:*key);
End-DS;
 // Assume File_C has key fields Custno and Invno

 // Method 1, using the Rec_Key data structure
 Rec_key.Custno = Arg_Cust;
 Rec_key.Invno  = Arg_Inv;
 Chain %kds(Rec_key) File_C;
 If %found(FileC);
   // Process found record here
 Endif;

 // Method 2, using a composite argument list
 // No data structure or key list is needed
 Chain (Arg_Cust:Arg_Inv) File_C;
 If %found(File_C);
   // Process found record here
 Endif;
```

*Listing 5-2: Chain operation alternatives with the %Found built-in function*

## *%Error*

Another built-in function available for Read and Chain database operations is the %Error built-in function. To enable this function, you must specify the operation extender (E) on the Read or Chain operation. The (E) extender tells the compiler that you want to handle file errors associated with the Read or Chain. Specifying the (E) disables the RPG default error handler for the operation. The %Error built-in function returns a value of data type indicator: '1' if an error occurred or '0' otherwise.

If you use the (E) extender, it is important to include some kind of error handling in your program. To do so, code an If %Error statement after the Read or Chain, followed by the desired error handling. The (E) operation extender provides the same function as placing an indicator in the low position of resulting indicators in the original fixed-format version of Read and Chain. If you place the (E) extender on a Read or Chain operation but do not test %Error, you are permitting an error to occur without action being taken. It is difficult to predict the harm that this omission might cause.

Listing 5-3 shows an example that uses the %Error function.

```
Chain(e) (Arg_Cust:Arg_Inv) File_D;
If %error;
  Exsr Error_subr;
Endif;

Read(e) File_A;
If %error;
  Exsr Error_subr;
Endif;
```

*Listing 5-3: Chain and Read operations with the %Error built-in function*

## %Equal

You can use the %Equal built-in function after a Setll operation to determine whether a record whose key matches the key list argument exists in the file. You can use a partial key in the key argument list as well. This combination can provide a valuable utility if the file being accessed has a multiple-field key.

For example, say you have an "on-order" file with a two-part key: customer number and order number. To determine whether a certain customer has one or more data records in the file, you need only code a Setll to the file, using the customer number as the argument, and then check the status of %Equal after the Setll. If the function returns '1', data exists for the customer, and the file pointer is positioned at the first record. If %equal returns '0', no data records exist for the customer.

Listing 5-4 illustrates using Setll and Setgt with built-in function %Equal.

```
// Assume EmpMast has a three-part key:
// Company, Dept, and EmpNo.
// To check for existence of a specific record by
// key but without chaining:
Setll (Arg_Co:Arg_Dept:Arg_Empl) EmpMast;
If %equal(EmpMast);
   // A specific employee record was found.
Endif;

// To determine whether at least one employee
// exists in a particular company and department
Setll (Arg_Co:Arg_Dept) EmpMast; // Set file pointer
If %equal(EmpMast);        // Check for existence
   // An employee record was found.
Endif;

// To set the file pointer to the next dept
Setgt (Arg_Co:Arg_Dept) EmpMast;

// %found will return '1' after Setll or Setgt
// unless end-of-file is reached
```

*Listing 5-4: Using Setll and Setgt with the %Equal built-in function*

## Data Area Input

Data areas, especially data area objects, could reasonably be called part of the database. You use the same data structures (definition specifications) regardless of the format of the calculations. Input from a data area is accomplished automatically, via the In operation, or by both methods.

# Database Output

The following operations perform output to database files: Write (Add a new record), Update (Modify an existing record), Delete (Delete a record), and, if you're using program-described files, Except (Exception output).

## Write

The Write operation adds a new record to a file. No prior read is necessary, but the file must be opened before you request the Write. An entire record is written with the Write, and you must take care to ensure that all fields are loaded properly before the Write. If new records are to be added to a file, the file must have either a file type of O or an A in position 20 to denote that you plan to add records to the file being read (file type I) or updated (file type U).

## *Update*

The Update operation works the same in free format as before. However, a new built-in function, %Fields, gives free-format programmers the option to update only specified fields instead of an entire record. You can do this in fixed format by using the Except operation and output specifications, but the %Fields function is not available to fixed-format users of Update. Without the %Fields option, the entire record is modified using the current values of the fields defined in the record.

For an update to succeed, you must specify U (for update) on the file declaration, and a successful Read (or Chain) of a record must occur. During the time between the successful Read (or Chain) and the Update operation, the record is locked. No other user can access the record for update until the update is performed, another record is read, or an Unlock operation is performed. Be aware that record locking provides a needed function to maintain data integrity, but unless you program carefully, it can create operational grief.

## *Delete*

The Delete operation removes a record from a file. If you specify no search argument, the operation deletes the record that was most recently read by a Read or Chain operation. If you specify a search argument (a relative record number or key), the compiler uses the argument to locate the record to delete. For files using a key, free format lets you use the %Kds built-in function or an in-line composite list instead of the fixed-format Klist to specify the search key.

To verify that the Delete operation found and deleted the record, you should use the %Found built-in function after the Delete. Using the search argument, no prior read is needed. After a delete using a key argument, the file pointer is positioned to the next record after the deleted one.

## *Except*

The Except operation uses a label to specify which output in output specifications to perform. The output specifications have a matching label on Exception output records. The function of Except output is identical to that in fixed-format calculations.

Listing 5-5 shows some sample database output operations and their built-in functions.

```
     // Write a new record in a file
     Write Record_A;

     // Update an entire record
     Update Record_A;

     // Update only certain fields in the record
     Update Record_A %fields(Name:Zip:Amount_Due);

     // Delete the last record read
     Delete Record_A;

     // Delete a record using a key
     Delete (Arg_1:Arg_2) Record_A;
     If not %found;
       Message = 'Record was not deleted';
     Endif;

     // Perform Exception output
     Except Label_A;
```

*Listing 5-5: Database output operations and built-in functions*

# Workstation I/O

To perform workstation input and output in free format, you use the same methods as in fixed format. The only difference is where you place the operation code and parameters in the free-format source statement.

## *Write/Read*

The most common operation to a workstation device is the Exfmt (Write then read) operation. The write portion of this operation moves the data from the specified record to the buffer of the display device's open data path. The device function manager checks the option indicators and performs the selected options, such as setting display attributes, displaying error messages, or performing keyword functions.

The read part of the Exfmt operation sends the output buffer to the device and then waits for input from the device. The input occurs when the user presses either Enter or an enabled function key. The operating system handles non-enabled function keys by returning a message informing the user that the key is not available.

## Write

The Write operation usually is associated with a display file for which an overlay function is needed—for example, for a trailer record preceding a subfile control record or a message subfile record preceding a regular display format.

## Read

We seldom use the Read operation in a display file. You can execute it immediately after a Write operation, but programmers usually use the Exfmt operation to perform this combination. Read is more commonly used when the specified file is an Intersystem Communications Facility (ICF) file.

## ICF I/O

RPG IV supports ICF files by letting you specify device WORKSTN in the file declaration. The RPG operation codes that you specify dictate what the communications device will do. The file declaration includes a device name (Dev) keyword, which ICF requires. The value of this keyword corresponds to the device entry names in the ICF file.

An Exfmt operation to an ICF record becomes a three-function combination: send a record, send a "turnaround" instruction to the other station, and then receive a record from the other station. The Write operation is simply a send-record operation. The Read operation with a record format is a receive operation. If the Invite keyword (DDS in the ICF file) was used previously on a Write operation, a Read operation using the ICF file name becomes a read-from-invited-devices operation. In communications lingo, this means that any device in the device file (that has been invited) may now send to the program. With this kind of Read, you can specify a record wait time limit that, if reached, can cause control to return to the program along with a time-out exception.

## Dsply

The Dsply operation is available in free format to provide the same functionality as its fixed-format counterpart. Because this operation comes from an original RPG format, you must remember to code the operation Dsply first, followed by Factor 1 information and then Factor 2 information.

Listing 5-6 shows examples of workstation I/O using free-format RPG IV.

```
// The following Exfmt sends the "Prompt" record to the
// workstation and waits for the response.

Exfmt Prompt Display_F;


// The Write operation sends a record to a buffer. The
// requested functions are performed, but data is not
// displayed now. In subfile programming, a "Trailer"
// record is written before issuing a write/read for
// the "Control" record.

Write Trailer;
Exfmt Control;


// Using Intersystem Communications Facility (ICF), a Read
// is used (by file name) to access data from any invited
// communications device. The file is an ICF file and uses
// the Workstn device in the RPG IV file declaration.

Read(e) Comm_File;

// After the Read, either a data record has been received
// or a time-out has occurred. You can use the %error
// error built-in to determine which is the case


// The Dsply operation lets you communicate with the user.
// The operation can display a message and accept a response
// to an interactive user or to the system operator if
// running in batch. The following question will be sent to
// the external message queue, and the response will be
// returned in field Food.

Dsply ('What''s for Lunch?') ' ' Food;
```

*Listing 5-6: Workstation I/O operations available in free format*

# Printer Output

In free-format RPG IV, you code printer output, whether program-described or externally described, the same way you do in fixed format.

## Overflow Indicator

The overflow indicator has been with RPG for a long time. Indicators OA–OG and OV have served us well. In RPG IV, an externally described printer file can use any numeric indicator. As of V5R1, you can also use a named indicator. This feature can make RPG IV programs that use printer files easier to read and maintain. The named or numbered indicator is automatically set to *On when printing occurs on or after the overflow line specified in the printer file definition. You can change the overflow line permanently by using the CHGPRTF (Change Printer File) CL command, or you can change it temporarily by using the OVRPRTF (Override with Printer File) command.

## Write

The Write operation uses a record name defined in the printer file and causes all output for the record to be printed.

## Except

You can use the Except operation with program-described printer files to print using output specifications. Program-described printing provides nearly all the functionality of externally described printing.

Listing 5-7 shows examples of printer output using free-format RPG IV.

```
// An externally described printer file PrintFile
Dcl-F PrintFile Printer Oflind(Ofl_1);
Dcl-s Ofl_1 Ind;

// To print all lines described by record Headings
Write Headings;

// To check for overflow and redo headings
If Ofl_1;
  Write Headings;
  Clear Ofl_1;
Endif;
```
*Continued*

```
      // To print a line described by record Detail
      Write Detail;


      // A program-described printer file Qprint
      Dcl-F FQprint Printer(120) Oflind(Ofl_2);
      Dcl-S Ofl_2 Ind;

      // To print using tag Hdgs on output specs
      Except Hdgs;

      // To check for overflow and redo headings
      If Ofl_2;
        Except Hdgs;
        Clear Ofl_2;
      Endif;

      // To print a detail line using tag Detail
      Except Detail;
```

*Listing 5-7: Output operations in free format*

# 6

# Program Flow
# Using Free Format

In nearly every program you write, you need to control the flow of instructions.
Free-format RPG IV offers experienced RPG programmers a new style for
controlling program flow. In this chapter, we look at the numerous operations
available for controlling flow in free format through conditional and selection
logic, "do" functionality, and loop interrupts.

## The If Group

Four free-format operations—If, Else, Elseif, and Endif—help you construct
programs that execute conditional logic in a structured way. Together, these
operations form a powerful arsenal for managing the flow of instructions in
your program.

## *If*

Since IBM modified the If operation for the extended Factor 2 format, this
operation has become a favored method for coding conditional logic. Rather
than write the following:

```
        A          IFGT        B
        C          ANDLT       D
```

it makes more sense to code

```
        If A > B and C < D;
```

To use the If operation in free format, just take the extended Factor 2 expression and assume you have the freedom to put it anywhere in positions 8–80. For every If, you must also code a corresponding Endif. The generic End operation (used in fixed format) is not available.

The If operation performs exactly like its extended Factor 2, fixed-format counterpart. The compiler checks factors in the comparison expression according to the operators given and the dictates of precedence (order of checking). The order of checking is as follows:

1. Complete checking is performed to true or false within parentheses.

2. When no parentheses are present, ANDs are checked before ORs.

If the premise expression of the If statement resolves to true, the operations that follow the statement are performed. The program continues with any number of operations until it reaches an Else, Elseif, or Endif statement.

If the premise expression resolves to false, program control passes to the Elseif premise, if present, or to an Else statement, if coded. If the If block includes neither an Elseif nor an Else, program control passes to the next operation after the Endif.

Listing 6-1 shows an example of If precedence.

```
// Consider the following If expression:

If  (Acctbal > 1000 or Status = 'A')
                and Date_1 > Date_2;

// Due to the higher precedence of parentheses,
// the logic group inside the parentheses will be
// resolved first. If either comparison is true,
// the group is true. If the group is true, the next
// part of the expression is checked. If this
// expression is also true, the If resolves to true.

// Now consider the same expression without the
// parentheses:

If  Acctbal > 1000 or Status = 'A'
                and Date_1 > Date_2;

// This time, with no parentheses, the "and" has the
// highest precedence, so the Status check is now
// paired with the date comparison. If Acctbal is
// greater than 1000, the entire If is true; if
// false, both the Status check and the date
// comparison must be true.
```

*Listing 6-1: Precedence in If comparison expressions*

Free-format's greatest advantage for If (and other program-control operations) is the option to indent subordinate program logic. Indenting gives your program a pseudo-formatted look, entirely the same as in other contemporary languages, and it makes the flow of the program's logic easier to discern. Listing 6-2 illustrates this method.

```
If Status = 'A' and Amount > 100;
   OK_Record = *On;
   Total_Amount += Amount;
Else;
   Count_No += 1;
Endif;
```

*Listing 6-2: If logic using indenting*

## Else

Most of the time, you won't need an Else operation, but Else (as well as Elseif) is available to handle the "false" leg of programming logic when you need to do so. If the premise of an If expression is false and you have coded an Else operation, program control passes to the first operation after the Else operation.

Just as with If, any number of operations can follow the Else. Indenting the operations specified after the Else gives future readers of your program a visual cue to the logic being used in the program.

## Elseif

The Elseif operation is a relative newcomer to RPG IV. It replaces the combination of Else followed immediately by another If operation. By using If with Elseif, you form a control structure that lets only one group of operations be performed. If the group includes no Else, it is possible that no group will be performed. By coding an Else operation at the end of the group, you create an option for the condition "none of the above."

## Endif

As I have noted, each If operation must conclude with an Endif. Free-format RPG IV provides no generic End operation like that in fixed format. The new approach makes your code "tighter" in the sense that only specified "end" operations work, reducing the chance of accidental error or misunderstanding by a future reader.

Listing 6-3 shows examples of If used with Elseif, Else, and Endif.

```
   If Action = 'A';
     Write Record_a;
     Message = 'Record added';
   Elseif Action = 'C';
     Update Record_a;
     Message = 'Record updated';
   Elseif Action = 'D';
     Delete Record_a;
     Message = 'Record deleted';
   Else;
     Message = 'Invalid action code entered.';
   Endif;
```

Listing 6-3: Using If, Elseif, Else, and Endif operations

# The Do Operations

Free-format RPG IV provides two Do operations: Dow (Do while) and Dou (Do until). Although the fixed form of the Do operation isn't available in free format, the For operation (covered later in this chapter) contains all the functionality of Do.

## Do While

The Dow operation uses a comparison expression, similar to the If operation. The expression is evaluated, and when it is found to be true, program control continues on the next line after the Dow operation. Any number of operations may follow the Dow operation.

The Dow operation has a looping control point at an Enddo operation. (Remember, no generic End operation exists in free format.) At the Enddo, program control is immediately returned to the Dow operation. The comparison expression is then checked again; if it is true, program control continues on the next line following the Dow.

As long as the Dow comparison expression resolves to true, the program continues in a loop. When the expression resolves to false, program control jumps to the first operation after the Enddo that is paired with the Dow operation, ending the loop.

With most Dow groups, a loop-control condition is set just prior to the group and near the end of the group, just before the Enddo operation. Listing 6-4 shows an example of a file read loop that uses Dow.

```
    Read File_A;                    // Initial Read
    Dow not %eof(File_A);           // Test here

      // Process record here when Dow test is true

      Read File_A;                  // Subsequent Reads
    Enddo;                          // Go back to the Dow
    // Control comes here when the test at Dow is false
```

Listing 6-4: Using Do while (Dow) to read a file until end-of-file

## *Do Until*

Like the If and Dow operations, the Dou operation uses a comparison expression. Dou sets up a future check but otherwise does nothing. Program control flows immediately to the next operation after the Dou. The controlling condition of the loop is usually set soon after the Dou, and an If test is placed afterward to determine whether to continue in the loop. You normally place the Endif for this If just before the Enddo. If the If resolves to true, the program continues after the If, keeps on going after the Endif, and finally comes to the Enddo. At this control point, the Dou condition is tested. If the expression resolves to true, program control resumes at the next operation after the Enddo. If the expression resolves to false, program control "jumps" back (loops back) to the Dou operation.

Listing 6-5 shows an example of a file read loop that uses Dou.

```
    Dou %eof(File_A);        // Set up for test only
      Read File_A;           // Get record here
      If not %eof(File_A);   // Check for end-of-file

      // If not end-of-file, process record here

    Endif;
    Enddo;          // Test here. If false, go back to Dou
    // Control comes here when the test at Enddo is true
```

*Listing 6-5: Using do until (Dou) to read a file until end-of-file*

## *Dow and Dou Differences*

The difference between Dow and Dou—and it's a big one—lies in when the comparison expression is checked, as well as in the program-control action. Program-controlled looping is common, and programmers nearly always adopt one of these operations as their preferred method. In most situations, either approach will provide a satisfactory solution.

If you want to set the controlling condition just once, a do until is the correct form to use. A do while may be the better choice if prior programming statements have already set the controlling condition. Which do loop you choose will depend on many factors, but the biggest factor is probably personal preference.

# *For*

A For operation and its termination control point, Endfor, define a controlled-loop group of operations. The For group uses an initial specified index value, an increment index value (or default), and a termination value. You can specify the For group indexing to either increment or decrement the current index before checking to see whether the result meets the termination condition.

A For group uses an index variable, as in the following example:

```
For    j  = 1 to 10;
```

You must define the indexing variable in definition specifications as a numeric field large enough to handle the largest index value. This example specifies no increment, so 1 is used as the default. The loop termination value in the example is 10. If the value of index j is 10 or less, program control will continue to the next operation after the For. At the Endfor, control returns to the For operation, where the index is incremented (or decremented) and then compared with the termination value. If the index is greater than the termination value (if incrementing), program control jumps to the operation immediately after the Endfor operation. If the index is not greater than the termination value, control continues at the next operation after the For operation. The index used in the For group can be used within the group and changed if desired.

A For group can also start with an index value higher than the termination value and decrement until the current index is less than the termination value:

```
For j = 100 downto 1 by 2;
```

In this example, the index j has an initial value of 100 and a termination value of 1. The index in this case is 2. The first time through the For group, the value of j is 100. The next time through, j equals 98, then 96, and so on until j equals 2. When j equals 2, the For group is again performed. Control then returns to the For statement, where j is decremented by 2, yielding a j value of 0 (zero). Because j's value is now less than the termination value (1), control passes to the next operation after the Endfor statement.

Listing 6-6 shows some additional examples of For.

```
//     Indexing low to high:
// The following is a traditional bubble sort of
// an array. Variable n is the highest element to
// be included in the sort, and i and j are indexes
// of two For groups.

For i = 1 to n;
  For j = 1 to n-1;
    If Array(j+1) < Array(j);
      SaveElem = Array(j);
      Array(j) = Array(j+1);
      Array(j+1) = SaveElem;
    Endif;
  Endfor;
Endfor;

//     Indexing high to low:
// The following routine finds the position of the
// last s in a phrase. Phrase is defined alpha-40
// "She sells sea shells by the seashore.    "

For index = %len(phrase) downto 1;
  If %subst(phrase:index:1) = 's';
    Leave; // Loop interrupt, described below
  Endif;
Endfor;
// The variable index will be 32 at this point.
```

*Listing 6-6: Using the For operation for controlled looping*

# Loop Interrupt

The loop operations Dou, Dow, and For normally end when the loop's index termination requirement is met. There are times in programming when you need to escape from a loop—either all the way out of it or just to its next iteration. RPG IV's loop interrupt operations Leave and Iter perform these functions for us. (Remember, free-format RPG IV provides no Goto operation.)

## Leave

The Leave operation causes program control to jump to the next operation after the current Dou, Dow, or For group. The effect is equivalent to a Goto, but it occurs in a structured way. You may be thinking that this operation's purpose is primarily error handling. Not so. Let's say you are using a For group to load 10 records from a database into a subfile. However, after five successful record reads, you come to end-of-file. To exit the subfile load routine, you can just set up an "If end-of-file" condition and leave immediately after the Read operation.

The code in Listing 6-6 (above) uses Leave after locating a correct value in a string. Listing 6-7 shows a sample subfile load routine that uses Leave.

```
     // Load a subfile with the next 10 data records
     For I = 1 to 10;
       Read data_file;  // Get next record or eof
       If %eof(data_file);  // If eof
         Leave;           // Jump out of For loop
       Endif;

       // Load subfile from data record here

     Endfor;
     // Leave instruction sends control here
```

*Listing 6-7: Using Leave in a load routine to exit at end-of-file*

## *Iter*

The Iter operation is the other loop interrupt. Specifying Iter causes the program to jump to the current Enddo or Endfor operation (depending on which loop we are in), at which point the normal function of the Enddo or Endfor is performed. As with Leave, the effect is equivalent to a Goto, but, again, the action takes place in a structured way.

A good example of using Iter is what I call "one-at-a-time" error reporting on a data entry panel. If a panel allows entry of 12 different fields, any of which could be entered with invalid data, either we check them one at a time and loop back with one error message or we find all the errors and use a message subfile. To use the first method, just check each field. If the first field is okay, check the second, and so on. If an error occurs at any point, set up for the correct error message, and use Iter to skip all further error checking.

Listing 6-8 illustrates this scenario.

```
Dou Exit;
   Exfmt ScreenRec;    // Panel displayed
   If not exit;        // not exit
     If Field_1 <> [valid value]; // Field 1 check
       Message_F1 = *On;
       Iter;
     Endif;
     If Field_2 <> [valid value]; // Field 2 check
       Message_F2 = *On;
       Iter;
     Endif;

     // Continue with other 10 fields to be checked

   Endif;
Enddo;
```

Listing 6-8: Using Iter to skip to the next iteration

# The Select Group

The Select operation, with its corresponding operations When, Other, and Endsl, creates a procedural structure very similar to If, Elseif, Else, and Endif.

## *Select*

You code the Select operation on a line by itself, and it starts the select group. Following the Select, you can specify a When operation with a comparison expression. If the expression resolves to false, control is passed to the next When with its comparison expression. The false jumps continue until either an Other statement or the Endsl is reached.

The Other operation is optional. If all When expressions yield false, no action is taken within the Select group unless you have specified an Other operation. Other means "if none of the above" is true, perform the operations between the Other operation and the Endsl. If any of the When expressions is true, the operations specified between the When that is true and the next When (or Other) are performed, and control then jumps to the Endsl operation. In a Select group with no Other operation, either one set of operations is performed or no operations are performed. If the Select group has an Other operation at the end of the group, at least one set of operations will be performed.

Listing 6-9 shows an example of Select, When, Other, and Endsl.

```
Exfmt Screen;
Select;
  When exit;              // User presses F3 - exit
  When update_req;        // User presses F8 for update
    Exsr Verify_data;     // Verify data first
    If no_error;          // Data okay?
      Exsr Update_Rec;    // Go ahead and update
    Endif;
  When cancel;            // User presses F12 - previous
    Message = 'Function canceled by user.';
  Other;                  // Enter key pressed
    Exsr Verify_data;     // Verify data
Endsl;
// Control comes here after one of When's or Other.
```

*Listing 6-9: Using Select, When, Other, and Endsl operations*

## Operations Absent in Free Format

Many RPG programmers are acquainted with the fixed-format Cas (Case) operation and its two-letter suffixes EQ, NE, GT, GE, LT, and LE. These operations are not available in free format, but you can easily replace them by using Select and When operations with Exsr (Perform a subroutine) operations to call the subroutines.

As you have learned, free format also lacks a Goto operation. Doing without a Goto isn't such a bad thing. Programming style texts and magazine articles have argued nonstop for decades about the good and bad points of using a Goto operation. Rather than anguish over a loss of Goto freedom, let's look on the bright side: No Goto means no spaghetti code! Many of us have had to sort out programs written by programmers who used Gotos—here, there, and everywhere. It was nothing short of a miracle that the code even worked. Maintaining this kind of code is a programmer's nightmare.

In earlier versions of RPG, the use of Goto was pretty common. Now, Leave, Iter, and even LeaveSr (Leave subroutine) let us perform Goto-like functions in a clear and orderly way. Armed with these structured operations, we don't need a "real" Goto, just an understanding of these loop interrupters. The lack of a Goto operation forces us to think of ways to organize our program logic using structured programming techniques. The end result is programs that are easier to understand and maintain.

# 7

# Embedded SQL Operations Using Free Format

Embedded Structured Query Language (SQL) has been available to the RPG programmer for a long time. This chapter is intended to show you the differences between fixed-format RPG IV with embedded SQL and embedded SQL within a free-format RPG IV program. My assumption is that you already know how to code SQL statements. Only the differences between fixed- and free-format embedded SQL will be presented.

## Database and Embedded SQL

SQL allows a user a great deal of flexibility when working with a database. A user can affect a large number of records within a file with very little code. The strengths of a procedural language such as RPG IV are combined with the strengths of SQL when embedding SQL statements within a program.

### Fixed-Format Method

RPG source programs that contain embedded SQL have a member type of SQLRPGLE rather than RPGLE. This member type causes the SQL precompiler to be invoked. The precompiler modifies the /Exec SQL statements (mostly into API calls) prior to invoking the regular RPG IV compiler. The general rules to follow in fixed-format RPG IV are as follows:

- An SQL statement must be preceded by the precompiler directive C/Exec SQL.

- The SQL statement must be followed by another precompiler directive, C/End-SQL.

- The SQL statement can begin on the same line as the C/Exec SQL line, but most programmers code the SQL statement on a separate line.

- Access to host variables is accomplished by preceding the variable name with a colon (:).

- The SQL communications area is included in every program (in a data structure) in definition specifications.

- Each source line of the SQL statement between the C/Exec SQL line and the C/End-SQL line must contain C+ in positions 6 and 7.

- The SQL statement can be entered anywhere in positions 9–80. Position 8 must be left blank.

Listing 7-1 shows an example of an SQL statement in fixed-format RPG IV.

```
C/Exec SQL
C+    Declare C1 Cursor
C+       With hold
C+       For Select *
C+       From Myfile
C+       order by Field4, Field7, Field3
C+       For update of Field2, Field6
C/End-SQL
```

*Listing 7-1: Sample embedded SQL statement in fixed-format RPG IV*

A nice feature of fixed format is the ability to prompt (using F4) and fill in values on the prompt screen.

## *Free-Format Method*

While free format introduces some differences from fixed-format SQL, some things stay the same:

- The source member type is still SQLRPGLE.

- The SQL communications area (data structure) is included in every program, as before, in definition specifications.

- Access to host variables is also the same, achieved by preceding the variable name with a colon (:).

The following points detail the changes to embedded SQL when you are coding within a free-format section of RPG IV code:

- No C is placed in position 6.

- The SQL precompiler directive includes no preceding forward slash (/). The statement is just Exec SQL.

- No C+ is used on subsequent lines; continuation is automatic. If a character literal must be split between lines, include a "+" symbol at the end of the first line to indicate that the literal is continued on the next line.

- The SQL statement may be entered anywhere in positions 8–80, the same as any free-format statement.

- The embedded SQL statement is ended with a semicolon (;), the same as other free-format statements. This character replaces the End-SQL statement that fixed format uses.

- Prompting is not available.

Listing 7-2 shows an example of an embedded SQL statement coded in free-format RPG IV. It is the same statement that was used in Listing 7-1. The indenting in this example is done manually to aid the program reader. Multiple lines are used for the same reason, and to make it easier to make changes.

```
Exec SQL
   Declare C1 Cursor
      With hold
   For Select *
      From MyFile
      Order by Field4, Field7, Field3
      For Update of Field2, Field6;
```

*Listing 7-2: Sample embedded SQL statement in free-format RPG IV*

# 8

# Data-Manipulation Operations Using Free Format

Data, it seems, is never quite in the form we need. We perform operations on our data to convert it to the form we want. Free-format RPG IV offers a variety of methods for transforming data to suit our requirements. In this chapter, we explore those options, which include assignment statements, a large stable of built-in functions, and operations for converting dates and times.

## Assignment Statements

Chapter 4 introduced the free-format evaluation operation. Evaluate, whether coded with or without the Eval (Evaluate expression) operation code, is an important operation in free format. The basic form of an Eval statement is

```
Eval result = expression;
```

Explicitly specifying the Eval operation code is optional. When you don't specify Eval, the remaining part of the line becomes an assignment statement that takes the following form:

```
Result = expression;
```

In either form, the evaluate operation performs the functions specified in the expression on the right side of the equal sign (=) and assigns (moves) the expression's result to the variable specified on the left.

Free-format RPG IV supports assignment statements for numeric, character, date, time, and indicator data. In the following sections, we take a closer look at each of these types of operations.

## *Eval Operation: Numeric*

For numeric operands, the evaluate operation places the result of the assignment statement's expression into a numeric result variable with proper decimal alignment. Variables used in the operation's numeric expression can be any numeric data type, including zoned decimal, packed decimal, binary, integer (signed or unsigned), or float. The compiler takes care of any data-type differences by creating work fields. If the result of the expression on the right side of the assignment is too large for the receiving variable on the left, you'll receive an exception message at run time.

To specify half adjust, result decimal precision, or both for a numeric assignment operation, you must code the Eval operation code explicitly, along with the appropriate operation extender: (h) for half-adjust and (r) for precision. Listing 8-1 shows some examples of Eval and numeric assignment statements, including two half-adjust operations.

```
Dcl-S Num1 Packed(5:2) Inz(93.45);
Dcl-s Num2 Packed(7:2) Inz(13754.76);
Dcl-s Answer Packed(11:2);

// Addition
Answer = Num1 + Num2;

// Subtraction
Answer = Num2 - Num1;
```

```
// Multiplication (no half adjust)
Answer = Num1 * Num2;

// Multiplication with half adjust
Eval(h) Answer = Num1 * Num2;

// Division (no half adjust)
Answer = Num2 / Num1;

// Division with half adjust
Eval(h) Answer = Num2 / Num1;
```

*Listing 8-1: Eval and numeric assignment statements*

## Eval Operation: Character

For character data types used in assignment statements, the resulting character string replaces the content of the variable on the left unless the left side is substringed. The resulting character string is left-justified in the variable or substringed location. With Eval or assignment statements that use character variables, the operation sets the left variable (or substringed locations) to blank before moving the data. The option to "pad" with blanks is unnecessary because the Eval or assignment always pads with blanks—in fact, you can't stop the padding. Those of you familiar with fixed-format RPG's MoveL (Move left) operation will note that the Eval or assignment for character data is equivalent to a move left with pad.

If the resulting character string is longer than the receiving variable or substringed locations, the operation truncates the characters in the result string beyond the length of the receiving field. Listing 8-2 shows some sample assignment statements that use character data.

```
Dcl-s Field7 Char(7) Inz('ABCDEFG');
Dcl-S Field3 Char(3) Inz('QRZ');
Dcl-s Answer Char(5) Inz(*blanks);

// Longer field to shorter field
Answer = Field7;  // Answer = 'ABCDE'

// Shorter field to longer field
Answer = Field3;  // Answer = 'QRZ  '
```
*Continued*

```
      // Longer field to shorter field – EvalR
      EvalR Answer = Field7;  // Answer = 'CDEFG'

      // Shorter field to longer field using EvalR
      EvalR Answer = Field3;  // Answer = '   QRZ'
```

*Listing 8-2: Assignment statements using character data*

## Evaluate Right (EvalR) Operation

To provide a right-justification option for character-string assignments, free-format RPG IV offers the EvalR (Evaluate right) operation. All other rules of evaluate are followed. EvalR is equivalent to the fixed-format Move(p) (move with pad) operation. As with Eval, the pad function is inherent in EvalR. Listing 8-2 includes some sample EvalR operations.

## Eval Operation: IS,OC

That "IS,OC" isn't a typographical error. It's my attempt to create a new acronym for "Indicator Set, On Condition." IBM brought us this new "sort of" assignment statement early in RPG IV. In one RPG statement, it lets us test a condition and have a specified indicator set to *On if the condition is true. If the condition is false, the indicator or named indicator is set to *Off.

The first term in this new expression must be an indicator or a named indicator. The indicator is set to *On or *Off based on the truth of the condition statement that follows the assignment operator (=). You can test any condition that yields a value of the indicator data type (true = *On, false = *Off). For example, the following statement sets named indicator Sfldsp:

```
Sfldsp = Rrn > *zero;
```

It is equivalent to the following RPG code:

```
If Rrn > *zero;
   Sfldsp = *on;
Else;
   Sfldsp = *off;
Endif;
```

## *Evaluate vs. Move*

The Move and MoveL operation codes have been staples of RPG since the language's inception. However, free-format RPG IV doesn't support these two operations, either as operation codes or as built-in functions. As you've seen, the evaluate operation provides an alternative to these operations in free-format RPG.

Many differences exist between evaluate and the move operations. You can easily convert most move and move left operations to Eval, but due to some fundamental differences in the way these operations work, there is no simple solution to converting some moves to an evaluate. Chapter 11 addresses the Move and MoveL problems in detail and provides solutions to common problems that you may encounter when converting to free format.

# Built-in Functions

RPG IV provides a rich set of built-in functions, many of which target data-manipulation tasks. Built-in functions let us perform data-type conversions, substringing, concatenation, and many other operations. If you have data that you want to transform from one form to another, odds are there is a built-in function available to make the job easier.

In the remainder of this chapter, we look at the numerous built-in functions available to perform data-manipulation functions in free-format RPG IV. Table 8-1 lists these functions, along with a brief description of each one.

| Table 8-1: Built-in functions for data manipulation | |
|---|---|
| **Built-in function** | **Description** |
| %Char | Convert to character data |
| %Check | Check characters |
| %Checkr | Check reverse |
| %Date | Convert to date |
| %Days | Number of days |
| %Dec | Convert to packed decimal format |
| %Dech | Convert to packed decimal format with half adjust |
| %Decpos | Get number of decimal positions |
| %Diff | Difference between two date, time, or timestamp values |
| %Editc | Edit value using an edit code |
| %Elem | Get number of elements |
| %Hours | Number of hours *Continued* |

| Table 8-1: Built-in functions for data manipulation (continued) | |
|---|---|
| %Int | Convert to integer format |
| %Inth | Convert to integer format with half adjust |
| %Len | Get or set length |
| %Minutes | Number of minutes |
| %Months | Number of months |
| %Mseconds | Number of microseconds |
| %Replace | Replace character string |
| %Scan | Scan for characters |
| %Scanrpl | Scan and replace characters |
| %Seconds | Number of seconds |
| %Size | Get size in bytes |
| %Subdt | Extract a portion of a date, time, or timestamp |
| %Subst | Get substring |
| %Time | Convert to time |
| %Timestamp | Convert to timestamp |
| %Trim | Trim characters at edges |
| %Triml | Trim leading characters |
| %Trimr | Trim trailing characters |
| %Uns | Convert to unsigned format |
| %Unsh | Convert to unsigned format with half adjust |
| %Xlate | Translate |
| %Years | Number of years |

## Converting Decimal to Character

Often, data is in the wrong data type for what we want to do. Before IBM gave us built-in functions, we used a Move or MoveL operation to convert a decimal field to character. Free format provides no Move or MoveL operation, but the built-in function %Char does what we need. The %Char function takes a numeric operand and returns it as a character string.

The general form of the %Char built-in function is as follows:

```
Character_variable = %char(numeric_variable);
```

A quirk of %Char is that leading zeros in the numeric field are converted to blanks (the numeric field is zero suppressed). To convert the numeric field to a character string that includes the zeros in the result, use the %Editc built-in function with the X edit code. The general form of the %Editc built-in function is as follows:

```
Character_string = %editc(numeric_variable: 'X');
```

Listing 8-3 illustrates converting numeric data to character using these functions.

```
Dcl-S Num1    Packed(7:2) Inz(7544.22-);
Dcl-s Num2    Packed(5:0) Inz(00715);
Dcl-s Answer  Char(10);

// Convert a mixed number to character
Answer = %char(Num1);        // Answer = '7544.22-  '

// Convert a whole number with leading zeros: %char
Answer = %char(Num2);        // Answer = '715       '

// Convert a whole number with leading zeros: %editc
Answer = %editc(Num2:'X'); // Answer = '00715     '
```

*Listing 8-3: Converting numeric to character using the %Char and %Editc built-in functions*

## Converting Character to Packed Decimal

Converting character data to numeric assumes that the character data is numbers, with or without a decimal point, and possibly with a negative sign. The %Dec built-in function uses three parameters to convert a character string to packed decimal. The half-adjust version of %Dec is %Dech.

The general form of the %Dec function is as follows:

```
decimal_variable = %dec(character_variable:length:decimal_positions);
```

The function's first parameter is the character string to be converted. This parameter can be a date, time, or timestamp in addition to a character string. The character string can include a plus sign (+) or a minus sign (–) at either end, as well as a decimal point (.) or a decimal comma (,). You must remove any currency symbol, thousands separator, or asterisks from the character string before the conversion. The %Xlate built-in can perform this task nicely within the %Dec expression.

The %Dec function's second parameter is the length of the return value. The third parameter is the number of decimal positions in the return value. These two parameters can be literals or named constants but cannot be other built-in functions.

The examples in Listing 8-4 demonstrate the possibilities. Notice the use of two additional built-in functions, %Len and %Decpos, in this code. These functions retrieve the numeric result field's length (%Len) and number of decimal positions (%Decpos).

```
Dcl-s Char1  Char(8)  Inz('1342.77');
Dcl-s Char2  Char(10) Inz('-78 33 5 1')
Dcl-s Answer Packed(9:2);
Dcl-c lenA    %len(Answer);
Dcl-c dposA   %decpos(Answer);

// Convert Char1 to decimal using %dec
Answer = %dec(Char1:9:2); // Answer = 1342.77

// Convert Char2 to decimal using %dec
Answer = %dec(Char2:9:2); // Answer = 783351.00-

// To shift the decimal point, increase the length
// of the return value, then divide by a power of 10
// equal to the number of decimal positions.
Answer = %dec(Char2:lenA:0)/10**dposA;
// Answer now = 7833.51-
```

Listing 8-4: Converting character data to decimal using the %Dec built-in function

## Substringing

Using the %Subst built-in function, you can specify substringing for a "source" string (i.e., a string on the right side of the equal sign) or for a "target" string (i.e., a string on the left side of the equal sign). %Subst is nearly identical to the CL built-in %SST and is also similar to RPG's Subst (Substring) operation. The return value of %Subst is a character string. The function's three operands are a character string, a starting location, and a length. If insufficient characters are available in the string at the specified starting location for the given length, the compiler issues an exception.

To substring a target string, you specify %Subst and its operands on the left side of an assignment statement. The location and length become the new home of the data string that is being sent by the right side of the assignment statement.

Listing 8-5 shows examples of substringing.

```
Dcl-s String1   char(5)  Inz('ABCDE');
Dcl-s String2   char(3)  Inz('xyz');
Dcl-s Outstring char(10) Inz(*Blanks)

// Put String1 in Outstring, starting with the B
Outstring = %subst(String1:2:4);

// Outstring now 'BCDE      '

// Put String2 in Outstring, starting at pos 6
%subst(Outstring:6:%len(String2)) = String2;

// Outstring now 'BCDE xyz  '
```

*Listing 8-5: Substringing using the %Subst built-in function*

# Replace

The %Replace built-in function has no counterpart in CL or RPG operation codes. This powerful built-in uses four operands and has several capabilities. It can delete characters from a string (only), insert characters from one string into another string (only), and delete characters and insert characters. When inserting, all of the characters in the first parameter are inserted, regardless of the parameters specifying starting location and length. The big difference between %Subst and %Replace is that %Replace uses two character-string operands: a "from" and a "to." The resulting character string is the return value, so the operation modifies neither operand.

The %Replace function's third operand is the starting location in the "to" operand. The fourth operand is the length. Using a zero (0) length for the fourth operand enables the insert function. Using a null—that is, two apostrophes (') together—as the first operand enables the delete function.

Listing 8-6 illustrates use of the %Replace built-in function.

```
Dcl-s String1 Char(12) Inz('I ate eggs');
Dcl-s String2 Char(4)  Inz('corn');
Dcl-s Answer  Char(20)

// Replace only
Answer = %replace(String2:String1:7:%len(String2));
// Answer = 'I ate corn              '

// Insert characters in a string
Answer = %replace('4 ':Answer:7:0);
// Answer = 'I ate 4 corn            '

// Delete characters from a string
Answer = %replace('':Answer:7:2);
// Answer = 'I ate corn              '
```

*Listing 8-6: Using the %Replace built-in function*

## Scan and Replace

The %Scanrpl built-in function is new to RPG IV in V7.1. It returns a character string in which all occurrences of a scan string are replaced in a source string with a replacement string. That's a lot of function in a small package. The general idea of this built-in-function is to find a given small string in a larger string and replace all the occurrences with a replacement string. The replacement string can be smaller, equal to, or larger than the scanning string.

The %Scanrpl function uses five parameters. The first is the scanning string, the second is the replacement string, and the third is the source string. The fourth parameter (optional) is the starting location of the scan and replace, and the fifth (also optional) is the length of source string to be scanned/replaced. The default starting location is position 1, and the default length is the remainder of the source string starting from the starting position.

By specifying two apostrophes together for the second parameter, you can remove the scanning string from the source string.

Listing 8-7 illustrates use of the %Scanrpl built-in function.

```
Dcl-s ScanStr Cha(4)  Inz('Spot');
Dcl-s ReplStr Char(6) Inz('Lassie');
Dcl-s Source  Char(30);
Dcl-s NewSentence Char(30);

// Scan + Replace
Source = 'See Spot. See Spot run.';

NewSentence = %scanrpl(ScanStr:ReplStr:
                        Source);
// NewSentence is now:
// 'See Lassie. See Lassie run.'
```

Listing 8-7: Using the %Scanrpl built-in function

## Concatenation and Trim

The character string operator + replaces RPG's Cat operation code in free format. The + operator performs concatenation only; it does not trim blanks, as the Cat operation does. If you want to produce output strings containing several fields intermixed with constants and having a sentence or message look, you will need to use the %Trim built-in function.

The %Trim built-in function trims blanks in three variations:

- %Trim removes both leading and trailing blanks.
- %TrimL removes leading blanks.
- %TrimR removes trailing blanks.

Each of these three built-in functions uses a single character-string operand and returns the same character string without the blanks. If a character string contains an intermediate blank (e.g., 'San Antonio'), that blank is not removed.

Listing 8-8 shows examples of concatenation and trimming.

```
Dcl-s City  Char(20)        Inz(' Rio ');
Dcl-s State Char(15)        Inz(' Illinois ');
Dcl-s Postal_code Char(10) Inz('  61414    ');
Dcl-s Address_L4 Char(50);

Address_L4 =   %trim(City) + ', '
             + %trim(State) + ' '
             + %trim(Postal_code);

// Address_L4 = 'Rio, Illinois  61414'
```

*Listing 8-8: Concatenation and blank trimming using %Trim*

## *Converting Character to Integer*

Another helpful built-in for data-type conversion is %Int. The original purpose of the %Int built-in function (and its companion, %Inth) was to extract the whole-number part of a mixed number. The %Inth variation performs the same function as %Int and half-adjusts.

In a later release, IBM improved %Int and %Inth, letting the parameter be a character string or an expression. The character string can include a plus or minus sign at either end and a decimal point or decimal comma. Blanks, which can appear anywhere in the character string, are ignored.

The %Int and %Inth functions can also extract the whole-number portion of a floating-point variable. However, you cannot use a floating-point constant (e.g., 7.4E3).

You can use the result of a %Int or %Inth expression in a program wherever an integer is expected—in array indexes, length values, or loop parameters, for example. Be careful, though, because the result can be a negative integer.

Another built-in function, %Uns, is equivalent to %Int but works only with positive numbers. Its companion, %Unsh, performs the half-adjust function. As with %Int, these functions truncate all decimal positions. The %Uns or %Unsh function may be a better choice for setting array indexes, lengths, or loop parameters because the result is always a positive number.

Listing 8-9 shows examples of %Int, %Inth, %Uns, and %Unsh.

```
Dcl-s Mixed_Num Packed(7:2) Inz(4387.77);
Dcl-s Char_Num  Char(10)    Inz('-7795.68');
Dcl-s Answer    Packed(10:0);

// Using %int to get the whole number part
Answer = %int(Mixed_Num); // Answer = 4387

// Using %inth to half adjust
Answer = %inth(Mixed_Num); // Answer = 4388

// Usint %int to convert character to integer
Answer = %int(Char_Num); // Answer = 7795-

// Using %inth to half adjust
Answer = %inth(Char_Num); // Answer = 7796-

// Using %uns to retrieve the whole number
Answer = %uns(Mixed_Num); // Answer = 4387

// Using %unsh to half adjust
Answer = %unsh(Mixed_Num); // Answer = 4388

// The %uns or %unsh function can't be used with
// Char_Num because it is a negative number
```

*Listing 8-9: Using %Int, %Inth, %Uns, and %Unsh built-in functions*

## Extracting Size, Length, and Decimal Positions

Data manipulation would be difficult without the built-in functions %Size, %Len, and %Decpos. Free-format RPG IV programmers make frequent use of these functions, not only for the handy functionality that they provide but also to avoid future "bugs." Programs that use %Size, %Len, and %Decpos are less prone to error when changes are needed (similar to the keyword *Like in definition specifications).

The %Size built-in function returns the number of bytes of its first argument. You use a second operand, *All, with arrays, tables, and multiple-occurrence data structures to calculate the total size of these items. It is important to remember that the %Size return value is the number of bytes, not the length. For character variables, size and length are equivalent, but for most numeric variables, the size is a different value than the length.

The %Len built-in function uses one parameter, a variable or expression, and returns the length. For character variables, this length is the size in bytes. For numeric variables, it is the defined number of digits. Other built-in functions, such as %Subst and %Replace, often require the length of a variable.

You can also use the %Len function in For groups to condition the stopping point when iterating through positions in a variable. Coding with %Len gives you the flexibility to automatically change a variable or parameter value instead of using constants, thus avoiding the need to make many program changes when a variable's length changes.

Another use of the %Len function is to set the current size of a variable-length character variable. Use %Len on the left side of an assignment statement with the new length as the value on the right side.

The %Decpos built-in function uses one numeric (non-float) parameter. It returns the number of decimal positions of the parameter as an integer. The parameter can be an expression, but float variables are not permitted.

Listing 8-10 illustrates the use of %Size, %Len, and %Decpos.

```
Dcl-s Ary Char(8) Dim(1000) Based(Ptr);
Dcl-s Char2 Char(10) Inz('-78 33 5 1');
Dcl-s Answer Packed(9:2);
Dcl-c lenA   %len(Answer);
Dcl-c dposA  %decpos(Answer);

// Allocate dynamic storage space for 100 elements
Ptr = %alloc(%size(Ary) * 100);

// From Listing 8-4, converting Char2 and adjusting
// the precision to match the Answer field
Answer = %dec(Char2:lenA:0)/10**dposA;
// Answer now = 7833.51-
```

*Listing 8-10: Using %Size, %Len, and %Decpos built-in functions*

## Number of Elements

You use the %Elem built-in function with tables, arrays, or multiple-occurrence data structures to determine the number of elements. You can use this built-in function as a value in a definition specification keyword or specify it as a factor in a procedure operation. As with %Len and *Like, %Elem can help you avoid future errors (e.g., by using it to control loops). If the number of elements in the definition for an item changes, then the %Elem value changes throughout the program. Using this built-in function to control For groups and other program functions is a factor in good program design.

Listing 8-11 illustrates how to use the %Elem built-in function.

```
Dcl-s Arry1 Char(8)  Dim(30);
Dcl-s Arry2 Char(20) Dim(%elem(Arry1);
Dcl-s i Uns(5);

// Use %elem to control a For group
For i = 1 to %elem(Arry1);
  Arry2(i) = %subst(Arry1(i):4:3);
Endfor;
```

*Listing 8-11: Using the %Elem built-in function*

## Looking for Something?

Three built-in functions provide assistance in finding a character in a character string. The %Check built-in function works the same as RPG's Check operation code. For the function's first parameter, you specify one or more characters as a literal or named constant. This character list is also called a *comparator*. The second parameter is the character string to be searched. The third parameter, which is optional, is the position in the second parameter at which the search should begin. If you omit the third parameter, the starting position defaults to 1 (one). The %Check function searches the string (parameter 2), looking for the first occurrence of a character that is *not* in the comparator (parameter 1). If a character is found, the search ends and the return value (an unsigned integer) is set to the position in the string where the character was found. The function returns a 0 if no character is found.

The %Checkr built-in function is the equivalent of the CheckR operation code. It uses the same three parameters as %Check but by default starts at the last position of the second parameter. The search is performed from right to left until either a character is found that is *not* in the parameter 1 list or the end of the string is reached. The return value is set to the position in the character string where a character is found or to 0 if no character is found.

The %Scan function is another built-in that replaces an operation code—in this case, Scan. The %Scan function's first parameter is a search argument. It is a character string of one or more characters specified as a literal, named constant, or variable. The second parameter is the source string to be searched. The third parameter, which is optional, is the starting position in the second parameter for the search. If you omit the third parameter, the starting position defaults to 1. The %Scan function searches the source string (parameter 2), looking for the first occurrence of a character (or characters) that exactly matches the search argument. The return value is the position in the source string where the search argument was found, or 0 if no match occurs.

One feature of the Scan operation code is the return of multiple found positions (in one scan) into array elements. The %Scan built-in function does not provide this function.

Listing 8-12 shows examples of %Check, %Checkr, and %Scan.

```
Dcl-s String1 Char(10) Inz(' NM QP ');
Dcl-s String2 Char(10) Inz('Bubble    ');
Dcl-s Answer packed(2:0)

// Find first non-blank in String1
Answer = %check(' ':String1); // Answer = 3
// Find last non-blank, checking right to left
Answer = %checkr(' ':String2); // Answer = 6

// Look in String2 for 'ble'
Answer = %scan('ble':String2); // Answer = 4
```

*Listing 8-12: Examples of %Check, %Checkr, and %Scan built-in functions*

## String Translation

Another data-manipulation task performed in RPG is translating characters in a string from one character to another. The built-in function %Xlate replaces RPG's Xlate operation code in performing this task. The first parameter of %Xlate is the "from" character list. The second parameter is the "to" list. The function makes a one-to-one relative match between the "from" list and the "to" list. The third parameter is the character string to be translated. The fourth parameter is optional and defaults to 1 if not specified; it is the starting position of the translation in the character string.

The %Xlate built-in works as follows: The first character in the source string is compared with each character in the "from" list. If a match is made, the character in the "to" list with the same relative location as the "from" list replaces the character used in the search. If no match is found, the character in the source string is not translated. The output character (translated or not) goes to the return value string. The return value string is built left to right. The next character in the source string is run through the process, then the next, and so on until all characters in the source string have been processed.

Listing 8-13 shows a sample use of the %Xlate built-in function.

```
Dcl-s CMoney Char(10) Inz('$1,342.77');
Dcl-c Char_out '$,';
Dcl-s Answer Packed(9:2);

// Combine %xlate and %dec to get data conversion
Answer = %dec(%xlate(Char_out:'   ':CMoney):9:2);

// The %xlate function removes the $ and the ,
// leaving just the numbers and the decimal point.
// The %dec function converts this result to
// a decimal value.
// Answer now = 1342.77
```

*Listing 8-13: Using the %Xlate built-in function*

## Combining Built-in Functions

Using one built-in function within another built-in function may seem a little awkward at first. As RPG programmers, we have been conditioned to break down everything into one step per operation. That is the way RPG was designed at its inception in the early 1960s. RPG IV, though, lets us code character and numeric expressions in the extended Factor 2. There goes one step per operation, right out the door!

As you've seen in the code examples, built-in functions often permit a parameter to be the return value of another built-in function. And within the second built-in function, a parameter can be yet another built-in function. Where does this end? Good programming style dictates keeping built-in nesting to a minimum. Our C-language brethren have already hashed out these issues because they use many more functions than we do.

At one end of the spectrum is the practice of using only one function (in our case, built-in function) per line of code. Doing so makes programs easier to read, but it takes more "work" variables. The opposite approach is to nest functions as much as possible. This strategy cuts down on the number of "work" variables and total lines of code. Unfortunately, it also creates very complex program statements. Another problem is that the debugger utility will not reveal the values of nested built-in functions.

The solution for all of us lies somewhere in between: Use some nesting, but limit it to two or three levels. Although it is tempting to use more levels, we need to constrain ourselves for the sake of the maintenance programmers who must read and modify our code.

You can see examples of built-in function nesting in Listings 8-5, 8-6, 8-10, and 8-13, as well as in Listing 8-14 below.

```
Dcl-s MonYear Packed(4:0) Inz(0216);
Dcl-s WrkDate Packed(6:0);

// Goal is to get Month, 01, and Year in WrkDate.
//   Month and Year are in field MonYear.

WrkDate = %int(%subst(%editc(MonYear:'X'):1:2)
          + '01'
          + %subst(%editc(MonYear:'X'):3:2));

*Inlr = *On; // Wrkdate now 020116
```

Listing 8-14: An example of triple nesting of built-in functions

# Date and Time Operations

Date operations such as Adddur and Subdur came to RPG IV with the beginning of the date, time, and timestamp data types. Free-format RPG IV doesn't support these operation codes. Instead, new built-in functions are available to provide this functionality.

## Converting Numbers to Date and Time

To convert dates in a character or numeric data type to a date data type, you use the %Date built-in function. The function's first parameter is the character or numeric data (presumably a date) to be converted. If the data in parameter 1 is not correct, an exception occurs. The second parameter is the format of the input data. There is a limited list of the possible formats—all special values beginning with an asterisk (*). The format parameter is optional; if you don't specify it, it defaults to *ISO or the date format specified on the H control specification. The %Date function returns the date value as a date data type. To retrieve the system date, specify %Date with no parameters.

To convert time values in character or numeric data to the time data type, you use the %Time built-in function. The function's first parameter is the character or numeric data to be converted. If the data in this parameter is not correct, an exception occurs. The second parameter is the format of the input data. As with %Date, a limited list of possible time formats is available; again, all are special values beginning with an asterisk. The format parameter is optional; when not specified, it defaults to *ISO or the time format specified on the H control speci-fication. The %Time function returns the time as a time data type. To retrieve the system time, specify %Time with no parameters.

Although infrequently used, the %Timestamp built-in function is available to convert a character or numeric field to a timestamp data type. To retrieve the current system timestamp, specify %Timestamp with no parameters.

## Converting Date and Time to Character or Decimal

Two built-in functions that you learned about earlier are also available to perform date and time conversions. You can use the %Char function to convert a date or time data type to a character string. In this scenario, the function's first parameter is the date or time variable. The second parameter is the desired format, from the list of possible special values, of the date or time in the character string. The output will include date or time separator characters unless you specify a 0 after the format.

You can use the %Dec built-in function to convert a date or time data type to a decimal number. The function's first parameter is the date or time variable. The second parameter is the desired format, from the list of possible special values, of the date or time in the numeric output. (The *USA option is not allowed for time conversion.) Listing 8-15 shows additional examples of date and time conversion.

```
Dcl-s Date8 Char(8) Inz('12312014');
Dcl-s Time6 Packed(6:0) Inz(182443);
Dcl-s D8 Date;
Dcl-s T6 Time;

// Convert the 8-character date to a date data type
D8 = %date(Date8:*USA);

// Convert the 6-digit time to a time data type
T6 = %time(Time6:*HMS);

// Get the current system date and load it into D8
D8 = %date();

// Get the current system time and load it into T6
T6 = %time();
```

Listing 8-15: Examples of date and time conversions

## Date and Time Arithmetic

To perform date, time, and timestamp operations, you use date or time variables and one or more of several built-in functions. For date operations, you use %Days, %Months, and %Years. For time operations, you use %Hours, %Minutes, %Seconds, and %Mseconds. Each of these built-in functions has one parameter: an unsigned integer representing the duration for the function.

You can use another built-in function, %Diff, with date, time, or timestamp data types to calculate the difference between two date, time, or timestamp values. Timestamp operations can use any of the above built-in functions.

The %Subdt built-in function retrieves a desired portion of a date, time, or timestamp variable. The first parameter is the date, time, or timestamp field. The second parameter is a special value that identifies which portion of the field you want to extract: *Months, *Days, or *Years for a date data type; *Hours, *Minutes, or *Seconds for a time data type; and any of the preceding values or the value *Mseconds (microseconds) for a timestamp data type.

Listing 8-16 shows examples of date arithmetic using the date and time built-in functions.

```
        Dcl-s Date1 Date Inz(d'2015-06-04');
        Dcl-s Time1 Time Inz(t'14.04.45');
        Dcl-s NewDate Date;
        Dcl-s Newtime Time;
        Dcl-s Num6 packed(6:0);
        Dcl-s Diff packed(6:0);
        Dcl-s Month Packed(2:0);

        // Calculate a new date three months from Date1
        NewDate = Date1 + %months(3); // NewDate= 2015-09-04

        // Calculate a time five hours before Time1
        Newtime = Time1 - %hours(5); // Newtime = 09.04.45

        // Extract the month from NewDate
        Month = %subdt(NewDate:*Month); // Month = 09

        // Calculate various items
        Diff = %diff(Time1:Newtime:*seconds); // Difference
                                             // in seconds

        Num6 = %int(%char(%time():*hms0)); // Current time
                              // converted into 6 digits

        // A message string:
        String = 'The current time is ' +
                 %char(%time():*USA);
        // If it is now 1:15 PM, String becomes "The current
        // time is 1:15 PM"
```

*Listing 8-16: Using date arithmetic with built-in functions*

# 9

# Math Operations in Free Format

Support for extended Factor 2 calculations and basic mathematic symbols (+, -, *, /) came to RPG IV before free format became available. Free format offers us the added advantage of being able to write assignment statements without the Eval operation code, and it gives us about twice the space in which to specify mathematical expressions.

In this chapter, we delve into the details of math operations in free-format RPG IV, examining how to construct math expressions, perform accumulation and exponentiation, and more. We also look at some unique aspects of free-format RPG IV as it relates to other free-format programming languages.

## Expressions in Assignment Statements and Elsewhere

We create mathematical expressions by combining variables, constants, and symbols to specify the desired operations. Before RPG IV, each line of an RPG program could perform only one step. To handle more complex expressions, we needed work variables and many operations. Now, we can express even fairly complex formulas in just one or two lines in a free-format program, and we can most likely do so without using any work variables.

## Four-Function Math

Free-format RPG IV doesn't support the older operation codes Add, Sub, Mult, Div, and Mvr. In their place, most RPG IV programmers have learned to use the Eval operation and the mathematic symbols associated with basic four-function math. The plus symbol (+) replaces the Add operation in an expression; the minus symbol (–) replaces the Sub operation; an asterisk (*) replaces the Mult operation; and the slash (/) replaces the Div operation.

In fixed format, we used the Mvr (Move remainder) operation immediately after a Div operation to calculate the remainder of a division. In free format, we can obtain a remainder using the %Rem built-in function.

Listing 9-1 shows examples that use the new math symbols.

```
// Addition and subtraction
Answer1 = Field1 + Field2 - Field3;
//   If Field1 is 20.55, Field2 is 101.03, and
//   Field3 is 50.00, then Answer1 = 71.58.

// Multiplication and division
Answer2 = Field4 * Field5 / Field6;
//   If Field4 is 45.03, Field5 is 8, and Field6
//   is 7, then Answer2 = 51.46, assuming Answer2
//   has two decimal positions.

// Remainder
Remainder = %rem(Dividend:Divisor);
//   If Dividend is 725, and Divisor is 320,
//   then Remainder = 85.
```

Listing 9-1: Examples using free-format's math symbols

## Short-Form Math

In the early 2000s, RPG IV introduced some new math operators that reduce the amount of coding required to do simple accumulating, decrementing, and so on.

To perform an accumulation in fixed format, we would code either

```
C          Total     Add  Amount     Total
```

or

```
C                    Add  Amount     Total
```

Before the new symbols, we would have coded this accumulation in an evaluation statement as either

```
C                    Eval Total = Total + Amount
```

or

```
          Total = Total + Amount;
```

Now, we can obtain the same result with the following free-format code:

```
          Total += Amount;
```

Besides the += accumulative addition operator, the symbol combinations -=, *=, and /= are available. In each case, the variable specified on the left side of the operator becomes the first operand of the add, subtract, multiply, or divide operation, and the variable on the right becomes the second operand. The answer is placed in the left variable. Listing 9-2 shows some examples of these symbol combinations.

```
        // Accumulation addition
        RRN += 1;
        //   If RRN was 5 before this operation,
        //   then after the operation it is 6.

        // Accumulation subtraction
        Balance -= Payment;
        //   If Balance was 719.31 before this operation and
        //   Payment was 65.48, then after the operation
        //   Balance is 653.83.

        // Accumulation multiplication
        Rate *= 1.05;
        //   If Rate was 7.00 before this operation,
        //   then after the operation it is 7.35.

        // Accumulation division
        NewPrice /= 4;
        //   If NewPrice was 100 before this operation,
        //   then after the operation it is 25.
```

*Listing 9-2: Examples of accumulation math*

## Exponentiation

RPG has had the ability to compute the result of a number raised to an integer power for a long time. Programmers just used a controlled loop and multiplied a number by itself the required number of times. We could calculate whole-number powers up to the maximum size of a decimal number. In the "roots" area, only square root has been available, using either the Sqrt (Square root) operation or, in RPG IV, the %Sqrt built-in function. However, until RPG IV, we have had no easy way to calculate complex roots and powers.

In RPG IV, the exponentiation operator (**) gives the programmer complete capability to determine the root or power of a number. Performing this task manually would require logarithms. An exponentiation operation takes the following form:

```
answer = number ** power
```

The *power* operand can be a whole number, fraction, or mixed number; it can also have a negative sign. Listing 9-3 shows examples of exponentiation.

```
// Simple power and roots:
Area_Circle = 3.1416 * Radius ** 2;
//   The expression above computes the area of
//   a circle using the power 2.

Cube_Root = 8 ** (1/3);
//   The expression above computes the cube root
//   of 8, making Cube_Root = 2.

Future_Val_Annuity = Period_Amt * (((1+i)**n-1)/i);
//   The expression above computes the future value
//   of an annuity. i is the periodic rate, and
//   n is the number of periods.
```

*Listing 9-3: Examples of exponentiation*

## Precedence

*Precedence* is a short way of saying, in a multifunction expression, what the order of the math functions is. Parentheses (()) are available to help the programmer change the "normal" order of operations. The rules of mathematical precedence dictate that expressions enclosed within parentheses are evaluated first. The next function to be performed is exponentiation (**), followed by multiplication (*) or division (/) and then addition (+) and subtraction (-). Evaluation proceeds from left to right except for exponentiation, which is evaluated from right to left.

Listing 9-4 shows examples of precedence in mathematical expressions.

```
// The following expression uses no parentheses.
Answer = 21 + 10 * 3 - 30 / 3;
//   The multiply and divide are done first, so:
Answer = 21 + 30 - 10; // (Intermediate work)
Answer = 41;           // Final answer

// Using parentheses:
Answer = (21 + 10) * (3 - 30) /3;
//   Parentheses math is done first, so:
Answer = 31 * -27/3;   // (Intermediate work)
Answer = -279;         // Final answer
```

*Listing 9-4: Examples of precedence in mathematical expressions*

## *Mathematical Expressions Elsewhere*

Assignment statements aren't the only place where you can use mathematical expressions. You can include these expressions in If, Dou, Dow, and For operations, as well as in many built-in functions. This useful functionality eliminates the need to create unneeded work variables.

You should be aware, however, that some unusual results can occur when using this capability. For example, consider the following code:

```
Dcl-S Ary1 Packed(3:0) Dim(10);
Dcl-S Ary2 Packed(3:0) Dim(20);
Dcl-S Sum  Packed(6:0);

Sum = %xfoot(Ary1 + Ary2);
```

In this use of an addition expression as the parameter of the %Xfoot built-in function (which calculates a cross-foot, or sum of the elements of an array expression), the sum includes only the first 10 elements of Ary2, not all 20 as you might assume. Because the arrays have different dimensions, the sum option limits the %Xfoot result to the number of elements that the arrays have in common.

# Eval Differences in Fixed and Free Format

Being able to start operations in free-format's position 8 instead of Eval's extended Factor 2 location (36) is one handy difference between the free- and fixed-format versions of the Eval operation for mathematical operations. Starting an assignment statement further to the left lets us make better use of the available space in a program line. For more complex math expressions, free format can eliminate the need for the multiple lines required when using fixed format.

The ability to use indentation to organize the operations performed by our code is another important feature of free-format RPG IV. This technique makes programs easier to understand and thus easier to maintain.

Listing 9-5 shows some equivalent Eval code in fixed and free format.

**Fixed-format Eval with a long expression:**

```
C                   Eval      New_Amount = ((FieldA +
C                             FieldB) * FieldC)
C                             / (FieldD + FieldE)
```

**Equivalent in free format, making better use of space:**

```
New_Amount =((FieldA+FieldB)*FieldC)/(FieldD+FieldE);
```

**If logic in fixed format:**

```
C                   If        Month = June and Moon = Full
C                   If        Amount_due > *zero
C                   Eval      Special_discount = .13
C                   Else
C                   Eval      Special_discount = .07
C                   Endif
C                   Endif
```

**Equivalent in free format:**

```
If Month = June and Moon = Full;
  If Amount_due > *zero;
    Special_discount = .13;
  Else;
    Special_discount = .07;
  Endif;
Endif;
```

*Listing 9-5: Fixed- vs. free-format Eval calculations*

Free-format RPG IV brings a couple other differences of note to the Eval operation. As you begin writing calculations in free format, keep the following points in mind.

## Naming Variables

An interesting problem arises in free-format RPG coding that doesn't occur in fixed format. In free-format RPG, we must either be careful not to name our variables the same name as an operation code or we must use an Eval operation when the receiving variable is the same name as an operation code. This normally is not a problem because we seldom name our variables READ or MONITOR. But once in a while, we might have a variable named SELECT or IN.

For example, if we had a variable named SELECT (Alpha, 1) and we used it in an assignment statement, the code would look like this:

```
Select = 'A';
```

The compiler would issue diagnostic errors, not allowing the statement. The compiler would see Select—a valid op-code—and analyze the statement line accordingly. The alternative, which is valid, would be to code the line as follows:

```
Eval  Select = 'A';
```

## Semicolon

Although a previous chapter described free format's requirement for a concluding character, I thought that a little reminder here might be wise. In free-format RPG IV, calculation lines must end with a semicolon (;). If the elements of a line of code exceed the space available, you can continue the code to the next line. You don't need any continuation character in free format unless the continuation "break" occurs within a character constant string.

If you forget a semicolon, the compiler issues an error message. However, the message may not clearly indicate that the missing semicolon is the problem. As I have mentioned, you can continue lines without punctuation. Thus, a second line might be a continuation of a first. When the compiler finds information on what it interprets to be a second line—due to the lack of a semicolon on the first line—it interprets the second line's information as operands of the operation code of the first line. When you receive unusual compile-time messages, check near the line in error. The problem may be a missing semicolon.

# Free-Format Math in RPG IV

Free-format RPG IV has a style "look" that is very similar to C, Java, and several other languages. Programmers who have come to free-format RPG IV from experience in these other languages find the transition fairly easy.

In terms of basic mathematics, RPG IV offers some unique features that make it quite easy to use compared with other free-format languages.

## *Numeric Data Types*

Before RPG IV, RPG supported only three numeric data types: zoned decimal, packed decimal, and binary. Now, RPG IV provides more numeric data types than either the C language or Java:

- Zoned decimal
- Packed decimal
- Signed integer (3, 5, 10, and 20 digits)
- Unsigned integer (3, 5, 10, and 20 digits)
- Floating-point
- Double precision floating-point
- Binary (four-digit and nine-digit)

C's numeric data types are integer up to 10 digits, unsigned integer up to 10 digits, floating-point, and double floating-point. RPG IV's floating-point and double floating-point data types match the C language definitions. Java also uses short or long integers (up to 20 digits) and floating-point numeric variables.

The new numeric data types in RPG IV are conspicuously the same as the C and Java types. If you need a function that isn't available in RPG IV, you can simply call a C or Java program, passing the needed parameters. Having full integer and floating-point data types enables RPG IV programmers to communicate with programs written in these other languages.

Rather than ask which programming language to use exclusively in our work, we should embrace the best language for a given task and then interconnect the programs. Practicality does dictate, however, that we limit ourselves to two or three languages.

## Changing Data Type

Often, we need to move a value in one data type to a different data type, if permitted. For example, a numeric field stored in a packed-decimal type can be moved to a floating-point field. The reverse may or may not work, depending on the length of the receiving decimal field. An integer field can be moved to decimal. A decimal field can be moved to character. A character field can be moved to numeric if the value is only numbers.

Changing a field in RPG IV is especially easy. The language lets us use any numeric data types we like in an arithmetic expression and then move the result into the numeric data type of the receiving field. To change numeric to character, we can use the %Char built-in function. And the %Int (and %Inth), %Uns (and %Unsh), and %Dec (and %Dech) built-in functions let us change character to numeric.

# 10

# Call and Return in Free Format

Free-format RPG IV supports both dynamic and bound calls, but it does so in a new way that differs from what you're used to in fixed format. Free format supports neither the Call (Call a program) nor the CallB (Call a bound procedure) operation, and the related operations Plist (Identify a parameter list) and Parm (Identify parameters) are gone, too. Instead, the new CallP (Call a prototyped procedure or program) operation provides the functionality for both of these types of calls.

## Call Prototyped (CallP) Operation

In free-format RPG IV, all calls to programs and procedures require the use of a prototype definition. Coded in the data declarations of the program or procedure that makes the call, the prototype definition defines the call interface for the compiler and describes the parameters to be passed on the call.

## Dynamic Call

To prototype a dynamic call to a program, you code the Extpgm keyword on the prototype (PR) definition, specifying the name of the program to call in uppercase letters within apostrophes ('). In the calculations, the CallP operation specifies the name used in the prototype definition and the parameters to be passed to the called program. (I explain parameter passing further a little later in this chapter.) The general format of the CallP operation is as follows:

```
CallP prototype-name (param_1:param_2:...)
```

Listing 10-1 shows a sample use of a prototype to call a program dynamically.

```
Dcl-Pr Check_Date Extpgm('DATCHK');
    date packed(8:0);
    flag ind;
End-pr;

Dcl-S Yes_or_No ind;

CallP Check_Date(ScreenDate:Yes_or_No);

// The program DATCHK is called dynamically with
// two parameters: ScreenDate and Yes_or_No. The
// parameters in the prototype do not need to be
// named, but some type of documentation would
// be helpful.
```

*Listing 10-1: Using a prototype to call a program dynamically*

When coding the called program, you can specify both a prototype (PR) and a procedure interface (PI) in the definition specifications, or, at V7.1 or later, you can omit the prototype but include the keyword Extpgm (or Extproc) and the program parameter. The procedure interface acts as the "*Entry Plist" used in fixed-format coding. The prototype and procedure interface names must match the actual program name.

Listing 10-2 shows a sample called program.

```
Dcl-Pr ChkDat;
  Date packed(8:0);
  Yes_No ind;
End-pr;

Dcl-pi ChkDat;
  Date8 packed(8:0);
  Yes_No ind;

Dcl-s Today date;

Today = %date();          // Set today's date
If %diff(Today:%date(Date8:*mdy):*days)) > 60;
  Yes_No =*On;            // Parm date > 60 days ago
Else;
  Yes_No = *Off;          // Parm date not more than
                          // 60 days ago
Endif;
*Inlr = *on;
```

*Listing 10-2: Called program example*

The alternative procedure interface (V7.1 and later) would be the following, with the prototype specifications removed:

```
Dcl-pi ChkDat Extpgm('CHKDAT');    // Verify!!
```

## *Bound Call*

To specify a bound (static) procedure call, you code the keyword Extproc on the prototype definition. Because subprocedures can only be called "bound," you don't need this keyword for their prototypes. However, if the called subprocedure is in another module, the subprocedure itself must use the Export keyword on its procedure "begin" statement for the subprocedure to be available to other procedures.

Listing 10-3 shows an example of a bound call.

```
Dcl-pr AR0300R Extproc;
   Screen packed(5:2);
   DB      packed(7:2);
End-pr;

CallP AR0300R(ScreenAmt:DBAmt);
// With the Extproc keyword in the prototype,
// the procedure call is a bound (static) call.
```

*Listing 10-3: Bound call example*

# Parameter-Passing Options

Prototyped calls give us some flexibility in parameter passing that is not available in fixed-format calls. A variety of keywords are available for parameters specified on a prototype and procedure interface to control the way parameters are passed and used.

## Value

By coding the Value keyword, you tell the compiler that you want the value of the variable to be sent to the called procedure. When you use this option, the called procedure receives the information it needs, but it cannot change the value in the calling program.

The traditional RPG parameter-passing method is by reference. Reference means that the address of the variable in the calling program is sent to the called program. The calling program defines the storage for the variable, and if the called program modifies the passed parameter, the parameter's value is changed in the calling program.

When you use the Value keyword in the procedure interface of a called program, you instruct the compiler to allocate storage for the parameter. When the program is called, the value from the calling program is placed in the parameter's storage. Any updates to the variable are local to the called program.

# Const

The Const keyword on a prototype parameter provides several capabilities. As with the Value keyword, the called program may treat the parameter as read-only (if the Const keyword is also used on the procedure interface). If the called program does not use Const in the procedure interface to match to this parameter, and the variable used in the CallP operation matches the prototype in numeric type and size, the called program can change the parameter's value. In addition, to accommodate differences between the prototype and the variable (or expression) used on the CallP, the compiler will generate temporary fields to handle mismatches in parameter length, numeric data type, or both. This functionality eliminates the need for programmers to make up work fields to use on the CallP.

# Options(*NoPass)

Specifying the *NoPass option on a parameter means that the parameter is optional; that is, it need not appear on the parameter list of the call. If you specify *NoPass for a parameter, you must also specify *NoPass for any parameters that follow it.

# Options(*Omit)

You can specify the *Omit option on a parameter that is not required but happens to fall in the middle of a parameter list. To actually omit the parameter in the call, specify the value *Omit in the parameter list where you normally would place this parameter. To determine whether the parameter was actually passed, check the parameter's address (using built-in function %Addr) in the called program to see whether the address is equal to *Null. If the value is null, the parameter was omitted. Any attempt to use an omitted parameter in a called program will result in a runtime error.

You can specify the Options(*Omit) keyword in addition to the Const keyword.

# Options(*Varsize)

The *Varsize option in the prototype permits a character parameter to be shorter than the length defined by the prototype. (*Note:* No option or keyword is needed for a character parameter to be longer than the prototype value.) When you use the *Varsize option, the called program or procedure must determine how many characters were actually sent. You can accomplish this by passing another parameter containing the length.

The *Varsize option is available only when you pass parameters by reference.

## Options(*String)

The *String option in the prototype is used with basing pointer parameters. You can specify a pointer in the parameter list of the call, or you can use a character expression. If you use a character expression, a null (x'00') is placed at the end of the expression. Programmers use the *String option primarily when calling procedures written in C.

## Options(*RightAdj)

If you use the *RightAdj option on a prototype parameter, you must also specify either the Const or the Value keyword. The character parameter value will then be right-adjusted in the parameter field.

## Options(*Trim)

If you specify the *Trim option on a prototype parameter, you must also specify either the Const or the Value keyword. The character parameter value will be passed (using a temporary work field) without leading or trailing blanks. If you have also specified the *RightAdj option, the parameter is padded on the left with blanks. If *RightAdj isn't specified, the parameter is padded on the right with blanks. If the character parameter has a varying length, only the nonblank characters are passed.

Listing 10-4 shows examples of some commonly used parameter keywords.

In the first example, the customer number and order number are passed to the bound procedure by value. The called procedure receives the values and within the program can change them. However, the value changes will not affect the parameters in the calling program.

In the second example, the Const keyword in the calling program allows differences between the parameter definition and the variable or expression used on the CallP operation. Because the called program has matching Const parameters for the first three parameters, they become read-only. If a matching Const keyword is not placed in the called program, the called program can change the parameter in the calling program.

**Example 1 – Value keyword—**

*Calling program:*

```
Dcl-pr Ordprt Extproc('ORDPRT');  // ???
   CustNum Packed (9:0) Value;
   OrdNum Packed(7:0) Value;

CallP Order_Print(CustomerNo:OrderNo);
...
```

*Called program ('ORDPRT'):*

```
Dcl-F OrderFileIF keyed;
Dcl-pr OrdPrt Extproc('ORDPRT');
   CustNum packed(9:0) Value;
   OrdNum  packed(7:0) Value;
End-pr;

Dcl-Pi OrdPrt Extproc('ORDPRT');
   CustNum packed(9:0) Value;
   OrdNum packed(7:0)  Value;
End-pi;

Chain (CustNum:OrdNum) OrderFile;
If not %found;
   // Error routine
Else;
   // Process order
Endif;
```

**Example 2 – Const keyword—**

*Calling program:*

```
Dcl-Pr Wkly_St_T Extpgm('PAY483');
   St_Taxable packed(9:2) Const;
   St_Exempt  packed(3:0) Const;
   St_Extra   packed(9:2) Const;
   S_Tax      packed(9:2) Const;
End-Pr;

Dcl-S FTGross    packed(7:2)
Dcl-S StateAdd   packed(5:2);
Dcl-S StateExem  packed(3:0);
Dcl-S StateExtra packed(5:2);
Dcl-S StateTax   packed(9:2);

CallP Wkly_St_T(FTGross+StateAdd:StateExem:
     StateExtra:StateTax);
...
```

*Continued*

```
Called program:
      Dcl-pi Wkly_St_T ;
        St_Taxable Packed(9:2) Const;
        St_Exempt Packed(3:0) Const;
        St_Extra Packed(9:2) Const;
        S_Tax Packed(9:2) Const;
      End-Pi;

      Dcl-S New_Taxable Packed(9:2);

      New_Taxable = St_Taxable - (St_Exempt * 29.75);
      If New_Taxable > *zero;
        S_tax = New_Taxable * .05;
      Else;
        S_Tax = *zero;
      Endif;
```

*Listing 10-4: Examples of prototype parameter keywords*

# The Return Operation

The Return operation has been available in RPG for a long time to tell the compiler that a called program is finished with all operations and that control should be returned to the calling program. To close files and deallocate storage (in the default activation group), the called program must set the LR indicator to *On before the return.

The Return operation in free-format programs works the same as the fixed-format return. The operation has no parameters if it is being used in a main procedure.

## *Subprocedures*

In a subprocedure, the Return operation has two functions. The first is the "go back" to the caller, the same as Return used in main procedures. The second function is to use an optional variable or expression to determine the return value of the subprocedure. If the subprocedure has no defined return value (in the procedure interface), no variable or expression is needed, and Return merely moves control back to the calling program.

In fixed format, you place the variable or expression in the extended Factor 2. In free format, you code the variable or expression after the Return operation code and a blank, anywhere in the remaining area on the line. In either format, you can use multiple lines to specify long expressions. As with all free-format lines, the Return operation, with its accompanying variable or expression, must conclude with a semicolon (;). Listing 10-5 shows a sample free-format subprocedure with a Return operation.

```
Dcl-Proc DateCV67;
  Dcl-Pi *N    packed(7:0);
    Date6      packed(6:0);
    ErrorFlag ind;
  End-Pi;

Dcl-s Workdate date;

// Convert a 6-digit date of the format MMDDYY
// to long Julian. For date errors, return a zero
// date and an ErrorFlag set to *On. If no error,
// return the date and ErrorFlag set to *Off.
Monitor;
  Workdate = %date(Date6:*MDY);
On-Error *All;
  ErrorFlag = *On;
  Return *zero;
EndMon;
ErrorFlag = *Off;
Return %int(Workdate:*LongJul);

End-Proc;
```

*Listing 10-5: Sample subprocedure Return*

# Accessing APIs

Application programming interfaces (APIs) are (mostly) IBM-written programs that provide a useful function not native to a high-level language, such as RPG IV. You call API programs, via either dynamic or bound call, using parameters defined in IBM's API documentation.

Older APIs use parameter passing by reference—which was the only method available before RPG IV. Newer APIs use the parameter options explained earlier in this chapter and the CallP calling mechanism that is provided in free-format RPG IV.

Hundreds of APIs are available, and they put significant functionality within the reach of your RPG applications. I will mention just a few examples here to show you how to call APIs from within a free-format RPG IV program.

## *API Examples*

One of the most popular APIs is the QCMDEXC program. You pass QCMDEXC a command string and the string length, and the command is run. A typical use of the QCMDEXC API is to execute an override command and then open a file. Listing 10-6 shows an example of this use of QCMDEXC.

```
Dcl-F FileA Usropn;
Dcl-S OvrFileB Char(80) Inz('OVRDBF -
                            FILE(FILEA) -
                            TOFILE(FILEB)');
Dcl-Pr OVRDBF Extpgm('QCMDEXC');
   String Char(1000)    Const
                        Options(*Varsize);
   Len Packed(15:5)     Const;
End-Pr;

CallP Ovrdbf(OvrfileB:%len(OvrfileB));
Open FileA;
// FileB will be opened, due to the override
...
```

*Listing 10-6: Using the QCMDEXC API to override a database file*

Two other APIs, CEEHDLR and CEEHDLU, let you enable and disable an Integrated Language Environment (ILE) condition handler program. The CEEHDLR API registers (enables) the condition handler program specified in the parameters, and the CEEHDLU API unregisters (disables) the condition handler. You will learn more about these two APIs in Chapter 11.

APIs QSNDDTAQ and QRCVDTAQ perform access to data queue entries. API QSNDDTAQ puts entries into a data queue, and QRCVDTAQ removes the next entry in a data queue. Queue options include first-in first-out (FIFO), last-in first-out (LIFO), and keyed. Listing 10-7 demonstrates the use of these two APIs.

**First, you must create a data queue object, using CL's CRTDTAQ (Create data queue) command:**

```
CRTDTAQ DTAQ(MYLIB/ORDERS) MAXLEN(100)
```

**This program segment demonstrates sending entries to the data queue:**

```
Dcl-Pr SDQ Extpgm('QSNDDTAQ');
   DQ     Char(10)    Const;
   DQLIB  Char(10)    Const;
   Entlen Packed(5:0) Const;
   Entry  Char(100);
End-Pr;

Dcl-s Orderdata Char(100);
Dcl-s DQ        Char(10) Inz('ORDERS');
Dcl-s DQLIB     Char(10) Inz('MYLIB');

CallP SDQ(DQ:DQLIB:%len(Orderdata):Orderdata);
...
```

**This program segment demonstrates receiving entries from the data queue:**

```
Dcl-Pr RDQ Extpgm('QRCVDTAQ');
   DQ     Char(10) Const;
   DQLIB  Char(10) Const;
   Entlen Packed(5:0) Const;
   Entry  Char(100);
   Waittime Packed(5:0);
End-Pr;

Dcl-s Orderdata Char(100);
Dcl-s DQ        Char(10) Inz('ORDERS');
Dcl-s DQLIB     Char(10) Inz('MYLIB');
Dcl-s Waittime  Packed(5:0) Inz(-1);

CallP RDQ(DQ:DQLIB:%len(Orderdata):
          Orderdata:Waittime);
// The wait time parameter has the following meaning:
// A negative number means wait indefinitely;
// otherwise, the value is the number of seconds.
// to wait for an entry to arrive on the queue.
// Control will return to the program with or
// without an entry.
...
```

*Listing 10-7: Example of using data queue access APIs QSNDDTAQ and QRCVDTAQ*

# 11

# Solutions
# for Problem Situations

Experienced RPG programmers who are interested in free format have stumbled across some problem areas when trying to use free-format RPG IV. Many familiar operation codes are not supported, and some have no simple equivalent in the new RPG. This chapter provides solutions for these problem areas.

## Solution for the Fixed-Format MoveA Operation

One of the operations that free-format RPG IV does not support is MoveA (Move array). You can perform the equivalent function of MoveA, however, by using various built-in functions.

### History

IBM created the MoveA operation for RPG II programmers in order to solve a then-current need for character manipulation. At the time, no Scan (Scan string), Subst (Substring), or Cat (Concatenate two strings) operation existed, and RPG's built-in functions were still decades away. MoveA's purpose was to move a character field to an array defined as character with length 1 (one) and a number of elements equal to the length of the field. Inside the array, programmers could scan and change the field using array indexes.

By converting the field to an array, you could perform character searches (scanning) using the array lookup operation. The Lookup operation code returns the location found in the array in an index, allowing modification of the array element.

Using MoveA, you can load a field starting anywhere in the array, not just in position 1, to imitate a substring function. You can place multiple fields in the array, emulating the concatenation function. Character management is easy if the character locations are available using an index; in this case, the character locations are available in array elements. After performing all character-management operations, you can convert the array back to a field, again using the MoveA operation.

Another function of MoveA is to move array data to another array. In the implementation of this function, there is no recognition of array element boundaries. The sending array can start at any array index, and the receiving array can start at any array index.

## The Free-Format Solution

In RPG IV, if you must move a field to an array rather than manage the field using character-string built-in functions, consider the following solution:

```
Dcl-s Array Char(1) Dim (30);
Dcl-s Field Char(50);
Dcl-s i Uns(5);

For i = 1 to %len(Field);
  Array(i) = %subst(Field:i:1);

Endfor;
```

To move the array back to the field:

```
For i = 1 to %len(Field);
  %subst(Field:i:1) = Array(i);
Endfor;
```

In most cases, however, you won't need these two routines because RPG IV provides many good character-management built-in functions.

The free-format emulation of MoveA begins with the %Scan built-in function. Finding a single character or a small string within a character string is easy using %Scan. As an example, assume you want to locate the small string 'qu' within another string—say, within the string 'Albuquerque'. To do so, just specify

```
Location = %scan('qu':'Albuquerque');
```

After this line of code is executed, Location has the value 5. To find the second 'qu', you need some loop logic.

To replace one or more characters in a character string, you can use the %Subst, %Replace, or %Scanrpl built-in function. Here's an example: Say you want to replace all occurrences of 'i' in the character string 'Mississippi' with 'a'. You can use the following routine to do so.

```
Dcl-s Search_char  Char(1) Inz'i';
Dcl-s Char_string  Char(30) Inz'Mississippi';
Dcl-s I Uns(5);

i=1;
Dou i = *Zero;
  i = %scan(Search_char:Char_string:i);
  If i > * Zero;
    %subst(Char_string:i:1) = 'a';
    i += 1;
  Endif;
Enddo;
```

Another (and quicker) way to perform this task is to use one of the two built-in functions %Xlate or %Scanrpl:

```
Dcl-s Search Char(1) Inz'i';
Dcl-s New Char(1)    Inz'a';
Dcl-s Char_string Char(30) Inz'Mississippi';

Char_String = %xlate(Search:New:Char_String); // or
Char_String = %scanrpl(Search:New:Char_String);
```

To build a long character string from smaller strings, consider the following example of concatenation.

```
Dcl-s F1 Char(10) Inz('Now');
Dcl-s F2 Char(10) Inz('is');
Dcl-s F3 Char(10) Inz ('the');
Dcl-s F4 Char(10) Inz('time');
Dcl-s String Char(50);

String = %trim (F1) + ' '
         + %trim (F2) + ' '
         + %trim (F3) + ' '
         + %trim (F4) + '.';
```

## The %Subarr Built-in Function

The task of moving the data of an array to an array is a bit trickier than some of the operations examined above. Built-in function %Subarr helps get the job done.

Let's look at an example where an element of an array is defined as 100 bytes, and another array is defined as length 1 with 100 elements. We want to move all elements of the 100-element array (Array1) to the element of Array2 whose index is i. The fixed-format MoveA calculation would be as follows:

```
Dcl-s Array1 Char(1)  Dim(100);
Dcl-s Array2 Char(100) Dim(50);
Dcl-s i Uns(5);
Dcl-s j Uns(5);
Dcl Arx Like(Array1) Dim(100)
                    Based(Ptr);

C                 MoveA  Array1      Array2(i)
```

To perform the same operation in free format, you could use this code:

```
For j = 1 to %elem(Array1); // Loop  1 to 100
   %subst(Array2(i):j:1) = Array1(j); // Move 1 char
Endfor;
```

An alternative solution is to use the %Subarr built-in function and a based array template:

```
Ptr = %addr(Array2(i));   // Point to Array2 element
Arx = %subarr(Array1:1);  // Move array to array   Check!!
```

# Solution for the Fixed-Format Move Operation

The fixed-format Move operation has been around since the inception of the RPG language. This operation has many functions associated with it, most of which you can handle easily in free format.

## Breaking It Down

The general form of the Move operation is as follows:

```
Move      FieldS      FieldT
```

This operation moves the source field (FieldS), right-justified, to the target field (FieldT). The functions associated with this operation include the possible conversion of data type (numeric to character, character to numeric, numeric to date, date to numeric or character, and others). Differences in field lengths between FieldS and FieldT can lead to data truncation or partial filling of the target field.

## When Both Fields Are Character

If both the source field and the target field are of data type character, three possibilities exist:

- Both fields have the same length.
- The source field is longer than the target.
- The source field is shorter than the target.

If the source field (FieldS) is the same length as the target field (FieldT), the following free-format operation produces the same result as the Move.

```
FieldT = FieldS;
```

If the source field is longer than the target field, the following free-format operation produces the same result as the Move.

```
EvalR FieldT = FieldS;
```

If the source field is shorter than the target field and you want the "pad" (blank fill) option, then the previous line above produces the same result as the Move.

If the source field is shorter than the target field and you don't want the pad option, you can use either the %Replace or the %Subst built-in function in free format to provide the same result as the Move:

```
FieldT = %replace(FieldS:FieldT:%len(FieldT)-%len(FieldS)+1);
```

Or:

```
%subst(FieldT:%len(FieldT)-%len(FieldS)+1:%len(FieldS)) =
                         FieldS;
```

Or:

```
FieldT = FieldS + FieldT;
EvalR  FieldT = FieldT + FieldS;
```

Or:

```
EvalR FieldT= %subst(FieldT:1:%Len(FieldT)-%len(FieldS)) + FieldS;
```

## Data Type Differences

The preceding examples handle the case when the data type of both move fields is character. If one or both fields are numeric, you can use the %Char built-in function within the parameter list of the %Replace or %Subst built-in function to temporarily convert the numeric field to character. (For a reminder of how to convert a numeric operand to character using %Char, see Chapter 8.)

# Solution for the Fixed-Format MoveL Operation

Like the Move operation, the fixed-format operation MoveL (Move left) has helped RPG programmers perform many functions. You can easily handle most of these operations in similar ways using free-format RPG IV.

## Breaking It Down

The general form of the MoveL operation is as follows:

```
MoveL    FieldS    FieldT
```

This operation moves the source field (FieldS), left-justified, to the target field (FieldT). As with Move, the functions associated with the MoveL operation include the possible conversion of data type, and differences in field length between the two fields can lead to data truncation or partial filling of the target field.

## When Both Fields Are Character

If both the source and the target field are character, three possibilities exist:

- Both fields have the same length.
- The source field is longer than the target field.
- The source field is shorter than the target field.

If both fields have the same length, the following free-format operation produces the same result as the MoveL operation:

```
FieldT = FieldS;
```

The preceding assignment statement is also the correct solution if the source field is longer than the target field or if the source field is shorter than the target field and you want to pad (blank fill).

If the source field is shorter than the target field and you don't want to pad, the following free-format operation provides the same result as MoveL.

```
FieldT = %replace(FieldS:FieldT);
```

If one or both fields are numeric, you can use the %Char built-in function within the parameter list of the %Replace or %Subst built-in to temporarily convert the numeric field to character.

# Solution for the Case Operation

The fixed-format Cas operation is another common operation not supported in free-format RPG IV. This operation, too, is easily converted using free-format techniques.

The Cas operation is equivalent to both the Select/When logic structure and the If/Elseif structure. The only difference is that with Cas a subroutine is always performed when a case condition is found to be true.

Consider the following Cas group:

```
Option    CASLT   7      Addsubr
Option    CASEQ   8      Chgsubr
Option    CASEQ   9      Delsubr
          CAS            Errsubr
          ENDCS
```

You can easily code this same logic in free format using Select/When:

```
Select;
  When Option < 7;
    Exsr Addsubr;
  When Option = 8;
    Exsr Chgsubr;
  When Option = 9;
    Exsr Delsubr;
  Other;
    Exsr Errsubr;
Endsl;
```

You can also accomplish the Cas logic in free format using If/Elseif as follows:

```
If Option < 7;
  Exsr Addsubr;
Elseif Option = 8;
  Exsr Chgsubr;
Elseif Option = 9;
  Exsr Delsubr;
Else;
  Exsr Errsubr;
Endif;
```

# Solution for the Do Operation

The fixed-format Do operation is not available in free format, but you can easily replace it with the free-format For operation.

## *The Do Syntax*

You use the Do operation to begin a repeating group of calculations, specifying processing parameters in Factor 1, Factor 2, the result field, and Factor 2 of a matching Enddo operation. Factor 1 is the starting index value for the repeating group. Factor 2 is the index limit. When the index value exceeds the index limit, the Do group is not processed, and control passes to the next operation after the Enddo. The result field is an index variable that contains the "current" index value. Factor 2 of the matching Enddo contains the index increment value. If you omit Factor 2, the increment defaults to 1.

You can use conditioning indicators on the Do operation and the Enddo operation. To interrupt (exit out of) Do groups, you can set off the conditioning indicator of the Enddo or use the Leave operation.

## *The Free-Format Solution*

You can easily convert a Do operation to a For operation. The For operation takes the following form:

```
For index = initial_value To limit {By increment_value}
```

In addition to incrementing to a limit, a For group can start with a higher value and decrement to a lower limit. In that case, you use the following form of For:

```
For index = initial_value Downto limit {By decrement_value}
```

A For group ends with an Endfor operation.

Listing 11-1 shows a fixed-format Do group and its equivalent For group in free format.

**Here is a Do group to be converted:**

```
C       1           Do        10                      RRN
C                   Read      Datafile
C                   If        %eof(Datafile)
C                   Leave
C                   Else
C                   Eval      SFF1 = DBF1
C                   Eval      SFF2 = DBF2
C                   Write     SFRecord
C                   Endif
C                   Enddo     1
```

**Here is the free-format equivalent:**

```
For RRN = 1 to 10;   // Increment 1 is assumed
  Read Datafile;
  If %eof(Datafile);
    Leave;
  Else;
    SFF1 = DBF1;
    SFF2 = DBF2;
    Write SFRecord;
  Endif;
Endfor;
```

*Listing 11-1: Using a For group to replace a fixed-format Do group*

# Error-Handling Techniques

Another part of free-format RPG IV that requires some attention is error management. Using an indicator in the "low" position of resulting indicators is not possible in free format. Also, in free format, built-in functions replace many of the operations that could check for errors by using the operation extender (e). Free format thus requires us to employ some new methods for error management and control.

The automatic calling of subroutine *PSSR is still available in free format. Unfortunately, this function does not help with error recovery. For automatic calling of subroutine *PSSR, the return point that is used on the Endsr (End of Subroutine) operation must be '*CANCL'.

Use of the low indicator or the (e) operation extender lets programmers recover from error conditions. Either of these methods disables the default RPG error handlers, letting you determine "what to do" when an error occurs. Many programmers have combined recovery actions with the *PSSR subroutine (using If logic) to perform the appropriate actions for recoverable and non-recoverable errors.

To handle errors in free format, you use either a Monitor/On-error/Endmon group or Integrated Language Environment (ILE) exception handlers. Let's take look at both of these alternatives.

## The Monitor Solution

The Monitor/On-error/Endmon solution is easy to set up. For one or more operations that do not permit the (e) operation extender, first place a Monitor (Begin a monitor group) operation in the source before the operations for which you want to define recovery actions. After the operations, specify the On-error (On error) operation, along with one or more status codes or the special value *Program, *File, or *All. Last, follow the On-error line with the code that you want to perform in the event that the specified error (or errors) occurs. You can specify additional On-error processing for additional error status codes. The Monitor group ends with the Endmon (End a monitor group) operation.

If an error occurs while the program is running and the status code of the error matches one of the status codes specified on an On-error statement, the operations that follow the On-error statement are performed.

Listing 11-2 shows an example of using the Monitor operation.

```
Monitor;
  Read FileA;
  If Not %eof(FileA);
    Longjdate = %dec(%date(date6:*MDYO):*Longjul);
    Pointer = %alloc(many_bytes);
  Endif;
On-error 1211;
  // Handle "file not open yet" condition
On-error *File;
  // Handle any other file errors
On-error 112:113:114;
  // Handle date errors
On-error 425:426;
  // Handle storage allocation errors
On-error;
  // Handle all other errors
Endmon;
```

Listing 11-2: Using the Monitor operation to handle errors in a program

## ILE Exception Handler

Another option in error management is the use of an ILE exception handler. You register the ILE exception-handling program using API CEEHDLR and must specify the program status data structure and a procedure pointer. To remove the registration, you use API CEEHDLU.

Once registered, the ILE exception-handling program receives control if no detail-line error handling (low indicator or (e) operation extender) or Monitor group has been specified. The exception-handling program tests the status code and either handles the exception or percolates or promotes the exception to the next program in the program stack. You can define more than one exception handler.

To use this method, you must prototype the register and unregister APIs, specify the program status data structure, and write the exception-handling program. The following priority is used when you specify an ILE exception handler:

1. Error indicator (fixed format only) or (e) operation code extender
2. Monitor group
3. ILE exception handler
4. File I/O error subroutine and program error subroutine (*PSSR)
5. RPG default handler for unhandled exceptions (main procedure only)

The ILE exception handler option is convenient because you do not need the (e) operation code extenders or the *PSSR routine. Also, the exception-handling program can take different actions based on the status code of the error.

# 12

# Sample Programs

To give you a feel for what it is like to create programs in free-format RPG IV, this chapter presents four different programs written in the free-format style. Experienced RPG programmers will have no difficulty following the logic used in these small programs.

In these examples, you will see free-format features of RPG such as built-in functions, controlled looping, mathematical expressions, and Monitor groups put to work. By examining these programs, you will gain a good sense for the free-format style of coding as well as the improved readability and efficiency that it offers RPG programmers. For a complete listing of all the components of these programs, refer to Appendix B.

## An Investment and Loan Utility Program

The first sample program has two portions that run independently: a saving computation section and a loan computation section.

The saving part of the program accepts parameter data from the display station: an amount to be saved, an annual interest rate, and a number of periods. Two savings options are available. The first is a one-time amount invested over time, with no additions. The other is periodic savings of a specified amount.

The program can accept either option or both. The periodic savings formula assumes that the user pays the first amount now, not at the end of the first period.

The loan part of the program accepts parameters from another part of the display screen. The program needs to know the loan amount and the annual interest rate, and it can either compute the payment, given the number of periods, or compute the number of periods, given the payment. The utility also displays the total amount paid.

Listing 12-1A shows the utility's display screen, and Listing 12-1B shows the free-format RPG IV program.

Listing 12-1C shows the display after some data has been entered. From this sample display, we can derive the following information:

- The user invests a lump sum of $1,000 now at a 3 percent annual rate of interest. The user also puts $100 into the account each period, starting now. The total amount saved after 120 periods (10 years) is $15,323.49.

- The user borrows $200,000 at 6.5 percent interest annually and wants to know the principal and interest payment if the loan is for 360 periods (30 years). The payment is $1,264.66, and if payments are made over the entire 30 years, the total paid out is $455,277.60.

```
A100XXXC                    Investment and Loan Utility              3/14/15
JIM                                                                  14:35:42

                          Investment Computations

              Initial Investment Amount:    _____
         Annual interest rate (decimal):    .00000
                    Number of periods:      __0
          Investment amount each period:    _____

     Value of Investment at the conclusion:              .00

                          Loan Computations

                     Amount to Borrow:       _____
         Annual interest rate (decimal):    .00000
                    Number of periods:      ___
          *OR*       Payment Amount:         _____
                     Total of Payments:                  .00



         F3 = Exit       Enter to run
```

*Listing 12-1A: Investment and Loan Utility display screen*

```
Dcl-f IandL workstn indds(inds);

Dcl-ds inds;
  Exit ind pos(3);
End-ds;

Dcl-s Merr ind;
Dcl-s n Packed(4:0);
Dcl-s i Decimal(10:10);
Dcl-s FVsing Packed(11:2);
Dcl-s FVann  Packed(11:2);
Dcl-s PerRate like(InvAnnRate);
Dcl-s ThisPayment like(LoanPaymnt);
Dcl-s RemBalance  like(LoanAmount);
Dcl-s PerInterest Packed(7:2);

Dou exit;                       // Loop until F3
  Exfmt riandl;                 //    Bring up screen
  Clear Errmsg;                 //    Clear error message
  Clear Merr;                   //    Clear error flag
  Clear TotInvest$;             //    Clear investment total

  If not exit;                  //    Check for F3 - exit
    If (InvAnnRate > 0 and InvestAmt > 0) or
       (InvAnnRate > 0 and InvPerdAmt > 0); // All fields OK

      n = invperiods;   // Set n - number of periods
      eval(hr) i = InvAnnRate/12;  // Compute monthly rate
      eval(hr) FVsing = InvestAmt * ((1+i) ** n); // FV single
      eval(hr) FVann = InvPerdAmt * (((1+i)** n - 1)/i); // Ann
      TotInvest$ = FVsing + FVann; // Sum of single and annuity

    Elseif (InvestAmt > 0 and InvAnnRate = 0) or
           (InvPerdAmt > 0 and InvAnnRate = 0);
      Errmsg = 'Error on Investment parameters'; // Error msg
      Merr = *On;                                // Error flag
    Endif;

    Clear LoanTpaymt;
    Select;
      When LoanPeriod > 0 and LoanAmount > 0 and LoanAnnRat > 0;
        Exsr CalcPayment;
      When LoanPaymnt > 0 and LoanAmount > 0 and LoanAnnRat > 0;
        Exsr CalcNumber;
      Other;
        If LoanAmount > 0;
          If Merr;
            Errmsg='Errors on both Investment and Loan parameters';
          Else;
            ErrMsg = 'Error on Loan parameters';
          Endif;
        Endif;
```

*Continued*

```
      Endsl;

    Endif;
  Enddo;
  *Inlr = *On;

  // Begin subroutines

  //--------------------------------------------------------------

  //   Calculate a loan payment subroutine

  Begsr CalcPayment;
  Eval(hr) PerRate = LoanAnnRat / 12;        // Get periodic rate
  Eval(hr) LoanPaymnt = LoanAmount * (PerRate /
               (1 - ((1.0 + PerRate) ** (LoanPeriod*-1))));   ·
  Eval(h)  LoanTpaymt = LoanPaymnt * LoanPeriod;
  Endsr;


  //--------------------------------------------------------------

  //   Calculate number of payments subroutine

  Begsr CalcNumber;
  RemBalance = LoanAmount;
  Clear LoanTpaymt;
  Clear LoanPeriod;
  Eval(hr) PerRate = LoanAnnRat / 12;     // Get periodic rate

  If LoanPaymnt > 0;
    If RemBalance + (RemBalance * PerRate) - LoanPaymnt
                                      >= RemBalance;
      Errmsg ='Loan payment amount +
                  insufficient, please increase amount';
      Leavesr;
    Endif;

    Dou RemBalance = 0;      // Computation loop
      Eval(h)  PerInterest = RemBalance * PerRate;

      If LoanPaymnt <= RemBalance + PerInterest;
        ThisPayment = LoanPaymnt;
        RemBalance  = RemBalance + PerInterest - ThisPayment;

      Else;
        ThisPayment = RemBalance + PerInterest;
        RemBalance  = *zero;
      Endif;
```

```
       LoanTpaymt = LoanTpaymt + ThisPayment;
       LoanPeriod = LoanPeriod + 1;


   Enddo;
 Endif;


 Endsr;
```

*Listing 12-1B: Investment and loan utility RPG IV program*

```
A100XXXC                  Investment and Loan Utility            3/14/15
JIM                                                             14:35:42

                        Investment Computations

            Initial Investment Amount:      1000.00
         Annual interest rate (decimal):    .03000
                     Number of periods:    120
         Investment amount each period:     100.00

   Value of Investment at the conclusion:    15,323.49

                          Loan Computations

                     Amount to Borrow:     200000.00
         Annual interest rate (decimal):   .06500
                    Number of periods:    360
            *OR*     Payment Amount:       1264.66
                     Total of Payments:    455,277.60



      F3 = Exit       Enter to run
```

*Listing 12-1C: Investment and Loan Utility display with data entered*

# A Customer Inquiry Program

Our next program is a simple customer inquiry application. Listing 12-2A shows the starting display screen. Listing 12-2B shows the customer inquiry RPG IV program. After the user enters a valid customer number, the program displays a screen similar to the one shown in Listing 12-2C.

```
A100XXXC                   Customer Inquiry              3/14/15
JIM                                                      14:10:29

            Customer Number: _____




     F3 = Exit      Enter = Run Inquiry
```

Listing 12-2A: Customer Inquiry display screen

```
      Ctl-Opt option(*srcstmt);
      Dcl-F Custinqdf workstn indds(Inds);
      Dcl-F CustomerP keyed;

      Dcl-DS Inds;
        Exit ind pos(3);
        CustOK ind pos(50);
      End-DS;

      Dcl-s Date8 packed(8:0);

      Dou Exit;              // Loop until F3 - Exit

        Exfmt RCustInq;      //  Display the screen
        If not exit;
          Clear Errmsg;      // Clear error message
          Clear CustOK;      // Clear indicator
          Chain Custnumdf CustomerP;   // Get customer info
          If %found(CustomerP);    // Check for "found"
            CustOK = *On;           // Set indicator for customer found
            Date8 = CustDatMon * 1000000 + CustDatDay * 10000 +
                    CustDatYr;
```

```
        Dateout = %char(%date(Date8:*usa):*usa); // Get date
      Else;
        Errmsg = 'Customer Number entered is invalid, retry.';
      Endif;
    Endif;
  Enddo;
  *Inlr = *on;
```

*Listing 12-2B: Customer inquiry RPG IV program*

```
A100XXXC                    Customer Inquiry                  3/14/15
JIM                                                          14:19:16

                 Customer Number:     100

                 Customer Status:  A
                   Customer Name:  ABC Tool Company
         Customer Address Line 1:  1234 Elm Street
         Customer Address Line 2:
                   Customer City:  Chicago
                  Customer State:  IL
               Customer Zip Code:  60606 1313
           Customer Phone Number:  312 555-3567

              Customer Amount Due:  1,342.00
            Customer Credit Limit:  50,000.00

             Date Customer Began:  12/05/2005



     F3 = Exit      Enter = Run Inquiry
```

*Listing 12-2C: Customer Inquiry results display*

# A Customer Data Entry Program

The third sample program accepts customer information from an entry screen, verifies fields, and then adds the customer data to the customer master file. Listing 12-3A shows the initial display screen. Listing 12-3B shows the RPG IV program. Listing 12-3C shows the panel that is displayed if an error is detected as a user enters data.

```
A100XXXC                 Customer Data Entry                  3/14/15
JIM                                                          14:21:09

   1 ........          Customer Number:   _____

   2 ........                    Status:  _  (Can only be 'A' or 'I')
   3 ........           Customer Name:     _____
   4 ........           Address Line 1:    _____
   5 ........           Address Line 2:    _____
   6 ........                     City:    _____
   7 ........                    State:    __
   8 ........                Zip Code:     _____ ____

   9 ........            Credit Limit:     _____.00
  10........        Telephone Number:      _____

  11........              Begin Date:    __ __ ____  (MM DD YYYY)



       F3 = Exit    F8 = Write new record    Enter = Edit data
```

Listing 12-3A: Customer Data Entry display

```
Ctl-Opt option(*srcstmt);
Dcl-F Cstdatent workstn indds(Inds);
Dcl-F CustomerP keyed;

Dcl-DS * PSDS;
  Pgmq Char(10) Pos(1);
End-DS;

Dcl-ds Inds;
  Exit ind pos(3);
  Write_Rec ind pos(8);
  Cust_Num_Err ind pos(41);
  Status_Err ind pos(42);
  Name_Err ind pos(43);
  City_Err ind pos(46);
  State_Err ind pos(47);
```

```
  Zip_Err ind pos(48);
  Phone_Err ind pos(50);
  Date_Err ind pos(51);
End-ds;

Dcl-s State_Ary Char(2) Dim(50) CTdata Perrcd(10);
Dcl-s Date8 packed(8:0);
Dcl-s Workdate date;
Dcl-s Work_Num packed(5:0);
Dcl-s Err_Write ind;

Dcl-s wkzipc packed(5:0);
Dcl-s wkzipec Packed(4:0);
Dcl-s msgid Char(7);
Dcl-s lineno Char(2);

Dcl-Pr CLSend Extpgm('SENDMSG');
  msgid Char(7);
  lineno Char(2);
End-Pr;
Dcl-Pr CLClear Extpgm('CLEARMSG');
End-Pr;

Dou Exit;
  Write Msgctl;                    // Write Subfile Control
  Exfmt RCstdatent;                // Display entry panel
  If not exit;
    Exsr ClearMessages;
    Exsr Clear_Inds;
    Chain Custnum CustomerP;       // Check customer number
    If %found(CustomerP);
      Msgid = 'DTA0101';
      Lineno = '1';
      Exsr SendaMsg;
      Cust_Num_Err = *On;          // Customer number error
      Err_write = *On;
    Else;
      Clear Rcustomer;             // Clear DB record
      CustNumber = Custnum;
    Endif;

    If Custstat = 'A' or           // Check status
       Custstat = 'I';
      Custstatus = Custstat;
    Else;
      Msgid = 'DTA0102';
      Lineno = '2';
      Exsr SendaMsg;
      Status_Err = *On;            // Status error
      Err_write = *On;
    Endif;
```

*Continued*

```
If CustNM = *Blank;            // Name
   Msgid = 'DTA0103';
   Lineno = '3';
   Exsr SendaMsg;
   Name_Err = *On;
   Err_write = *On;
Else;
   CustNM = %trim(CustNM);
   CustName = %trim(CustNM);
Endif;

CustAdr1 = %trim(CustA1);      // Address Line 1
CustA1   = %trim(CustA1);      // Address Line 1
CustAdr2 = %trim(CustA2);      // Address Line 2
CustA2   = %trim(CustA2);      // Address Line 2

If CustCty = *Blank;
   Msgid = 'DTA0104';
   Lineno = '6';
   Exsr SendaMsg;
   City_Err = *On;
   Err_write = *On;
Else;
   CustCity = %trim(CustCty);
   CustCty = %trim(CustCty);
Endif;

If %lookup(CustSta:State_Ary:1) = *zero;
   Msgid = 'DTA0105';
   Lineno = '7';
   Exsr SendaMsg;
   State_Err = *On;
   Err_write = *On;
Else;
   CustState = CustSta;
Endif;

Exsr Check_zip;            // Check zip code & extension in subr

Custcrlimt = Custcrl;  // Credit Limit

If Custac < 99 or Custphn < 1000000;
   Msgid = 'DTA0107';
   Lineno = '10';
   Exsr SendaMsg;
   Phone_Err = *On;
   Err_write = *On;
Else;
   CustAreaCD = CustAC;
   CustPhone  = CustPhn;
Endif;
```

```
        Date8 = CustMon * 1000000 + CustDay * 10000 + CustYr;
        Monitor;  // Check date conversion
        Workdate = %date(Date8:*usa);
        On-Error *All;
          Msgid = 'DTA0108';
          Lineno = '11';
          Exsr SendaMsg;
          Date_Err  = *On;
          Err_write = *On;
        EndMon;

        If not Date_Err;
          CustDatMon = CustMon;
          CustDatDay = CustDay;
          CustDatYr  = CustYr;
        Endif;

        If not Err_Write and Write_Rec;  // Write new Cust Record
          Write Rcustomer;
        Endif;

      Endif;
    Enddo;
    *Inlr = *on;

    Begsr Clear_Inds;
    Clear Cust_Num_Err;
    Clear Status_Err;
    Clear Name_Err;
    Clear City_Err;
    Clear State_Err;
    Clear Zip_Err;
    Clear Phone_Err;
    Clear Date_Err;
    Clear Err_Write;
    Endsr;

    Begsr Check_Zip;
    Monitor;
    Work_Num = %int(CustZp);
    If Custzpe <> *blank;
      Work_Num = %int(Custzpe);
    Endif;
    On-Error *all;
      Msgid = 'DTA0106';
      Lineno = '8';
      Exsr SendaMsg;
      Zip_Err = *On;
      Err_Write = *On;
    EndMon;
```

*Continued*

```
      If Not Zip_Err;
        WkZipc  = %int(CustZp);
        Custzip = %editc(WkZipc:'X');
        Custzp  = %editc(WkZipc:'X');
        If Custzpe <> *blank;
          WkZipec  = %int(CustZpe);
          Custzext = %editc(WkZipec:'X');
          Custzpe  = %editc(WkZipec:'X');
        Endif;
      Endif;
      Endsr;

      Begsr Sendamsg;
      Callp CLSend(MsgID:Lineno); // Call CL Pgm
      Endsr;


      Begsr ClearMessages;
      Callp CLClear();              // Call CL Pgm
      Endsr;

**
ALAKAZARCACOCTDEFLGA
HIIDILINIAKSKYLAMEMD
MAMIMNMSMOMTNENVNHNJ
NMNYNCNDOHOKORPARISC
SDTNTXUTVTVAWAWVWIWY
```

Listing 12-3B: Customer data entry RPG IV program

```
A100XXXC               Customer Data Entry                  3/14/15
JIM                                                       14:30:48

  1 .......       Customer Number:    600

  2 .......               Status:  E   (Can only be 'A' or 'I')
  3 .......        Customer Name:  Jones and Smith, Inc.
  4 .......       Address Line 1:  225 Main St.
  5 .......       Address Line 2:
  6 .......                 City:  Madison
  7 .......                State:  WI
  8 .......            Zip Code:  53703 2811

  9 .......         Credit Limit:  50,000.00
 10 .......     Telephone Number:  608 555-6666

 11 .......           Begin Date:   9 16 2008    (MM DD YYYY)



        F3 = Exit    F8 = Write new record    Enter = Edit data
    Line 2: Status value entered not 'A' or 'I'
```

Listing 12-3C: Customer Data Entry error display

# A Sales Report Program

Our last sample program produces a sales report with several level breaks. Listing 12-4A shows the sales report looks like, and Listing 12-4B shows the RPG IV program.

```
Page 1                           Martin Widget Company
                            Sales Report for Sales Person    30


                          Customer Invoice                Invoice           Open
State Year Month Day      Number   Number                 Amount          Amount

  IL  2013  12    30        500     9051                1,000.00             .00

      2013  12             Total for Month:             1,000.00             .00

  IL                       Total for State:             1,000.00             .00

      2013                 Total for Year:              1,000.00             .00

  AL  2014   1    15        100    10010                2,000.00        2,000.00

  AL  2014   1    20        100    10050                1,500.00        1,500.00

      2014   1             Total for Month:             3,500.00        3,500.00

  AL  2014   2     7        100    10100                7,300.00        5,500.00

      2014   2             Total for Month:             7,300.00        5,500.00

  AL                       Total for State:            10,800.00        9,000.00

  CO  2014   1    16        200    10011                3,000.00        2,500.00

      2014   1             Total for Month:             3,000.00        2,500.00

  CO                       Total for State:             3,000.00        2,500.00

  ME  2014   1    16        300    10012                1,000.00             .00

      2014   1             Total for Month:             1,000.00             .00

  ME                       Total for State:             1,000.00             .00

  NH  2014   1    16        400    10013                  500.00          500.00

  NH  2014   1    17        400    10014                7,030.00        5,000.00

      2014   1             Total for Month:             7,530.00        5,500.00

  NH                       Total for State:             7,530.00        5,500.00

                                                                      Continued
```

```
=====================================================================================
Page 2                              Martin Widget Company
                              Sales Report for Sales Person    30

                        Customer Invoice              Invoice             Open
State Year Month Day     Number   Number              Amount             Amount
      2014               Total for Year:            22,330.00          17,000.00


                        Total for Person:           23,330.00          17,000.00


=====================================================================================
Page 3                              Martin Widget Company
                              Sales Report for Sales Person    40

                        Customer Invoice              Invoice             Open
State Year Month Day     Number   Number              Amount             Amount

 IA   2013  12   30        175     9053               730.00               .00

 IA   2013  12   30        175     9055               917.00               .00

      2013  12           Total for Month:           1,647.00               .00

 IA                      Total for State:           1,647.00               .00

 MN   2014   1   21        600    10060               145.00             145.00

 MN   2014   1   22        600    10061               850.00             200.00

      2014   1           Total for Month:             995.00             345.00

 MN                      Total for State:             995.00             345.00

 OH   2014   1   17        250    10015               325.00             325.00

 OH                      Total for State:             325.00             325.00

      2014               Total for Year:            1,320.00             670.00


                        Total for Person:           2,967.00             670.00
```

Listing 12-4A: Sample sales report

```
//----------------------------------------------------------------
// Program name: SalesRpt1
//
// Purpose:      Print detail sales and totals for each
//               salesperson
//               by year, state, and month.
//
//----------------------------------------------------------------
//   Define the files to be used

Dcl-F CustSls1l keyed;
Dcl-F SalesRpt1 Printer OFLIND(Overflow);
Dcl-s Overflow ind;

// Main Procedure

Read CustSls1l;

If not %eof(CustSls1l);

  SavePerson = SLperson;
  Write Headings;

Endif;

SaveState = SlState;
SaveYear  = Sliyy;
SaveMonth = Slimm;

Dow not %eof(CustSls1l);   // Do while not at eof

  If SlPerson <> Saveperson;
    Exsr Check_Overflow;
    Exsr Month_break;

    Exsr Check_Overflow;
    Exsr State_break;

    Exsr Check_Overflow;
    Exsr Year_break;

    Exsr Check_Overflow;
    Exsr Person_break;
    Write Headings;
  Endif;

  If SliYY <> SaveYear;
    Exsr Check_Overflow;
    Exsr Month_break;
```

*Continued*

```
      Exsr Check_Overflow;
      Exsr State_break;

      Exsr Check_Overflow;
      Exsr Year_break;
   Endif;

   If SlState <> SaveState;
      Exsr Check_Overflow;
      Exsr Month_break;

      Exsr Check_Overflow;
      Exsr State_break;
   Endif;

   If SliMM <> SaveMonth;
      Exsr Check_Overflow;
      Exsr Month_break;
   Endif;

   Exsr Check_Overflow;
   Write DETAIL;              // Print customer detail

   Exsr AccumDet;

   Read CustSlsl1;            // Read next record in the file

Enddo;

Exsr Month_Break;
Exsr State_Break;
Exsr Year_Break;
Exsr Person_Break;

*Inlr = *On;                 // End program

//-------------------------------------------------------------
Begsr AccumDet;

TL1iamt += Sliamt;
TL1oamt += Sloamt;

Endsr;
//-------------------------------------------------------------
Begsr Month_Break;

TL2iamt += Tl1iamt;
TL2oamt += Tl1oamt;

Write TotMon;
```

```
Clear Tl1iamt;
Clear Tl1oamt;
SaveMonth = Slimm;
Endsr;
//-----------------------------------------------------------------
Begsr State_Break;

TL3iamt += Tl2iamt;
TL3oamt += Tl2oamt;

Write TotState;

Clear Tl2iamt;
Clear Tl2oamt;
SaveState = SlState;

Endsr;
//-----------------------------------------------------------------
Begsr Year_Break;

TL4iamt += Tl3iamt;
TL4oamt += Tl3oamt;

Write TotYear;

Clear Tl3iamt;
Clear Tl3oamt;
SaveYear = SliYY;

Endsr;
//-----------------------------------------------------------------
Begsr Person_break;

Write TotPerson;

Clear Tl4iamt;
Clear Tl4oamt;

Saveperson = Slperson;
Endsr;
//-----------------------------------------------------------------
Begsr Check_Overflow;
   If Overflow;              // Check for and handle overflow
   // If true, print headings and reset overflow indicator
     Write Headings;
     Reset Overflow;
   Endif;
Endsr;
```

*Listing 12-4B: Sales report RPG IV program*

# Free-Format Operations

This appendix lists each RPG IV operation that you can perform in free format as of the V7.1 release of the IBM i operating system on IBM Power Systems. For each operation, the appendix presents the following information:

- The operation code and its name
- A model of the operation's syntax, showing operation extenders possible (in braces, or {}) and word descriptors (e.g., device-name) for operation parameters; optional parameters appear within braces
- A short description of the purpose of the operation
- An example of the operation

For a full explanation of each operation and its parameters, consult the IBM publication *ILE RPG Language Reference* (SC09-2508), which is available in the IBM i Information Center (*pic.dhe.ibm.com/infocenter/iseries/v7r1m0*) under **Programming > Programming Languages > RPG**.

## Expression Operators

In addition to operation codes, free-format RPG IV uses expression operators to perform operations that were previously performed by operation codes. The mathematical operators are as follows:

| Operator | Description |
|----------|-------------|
| + | Add |
| – | Subtract |
| * | Multiply |
| / | Divide |
| ** | Exponentiation (raise to a power) |

The character expression operator is as follows:

| Operator | Description |
|----------|-------------|
| + | Concatenation |

The assignment operator is as follows:

| Operator | Description |
|----------|-------------|
| = | Set equal to |

A combination of a mathematical operator and the assignment operator results in an "accumulation" function. For example, $a += b$ is equivalent to $a = a + b$. The accumulation operations are as follows:

| Operator | Description |
|----------|-------------|
| += | Accumulative add |
| –= | Accumulative subtract |
| *= | Accumulative multiply |
| /= | Accumulative divide |

Expression operators used for testing or comparing variables are as follows:

| Operator | Description |
|----------|-------------|
| < | Less than |
| > | Greater than |
| = | Equal to |
| <= | Less than or equal to |
| >= | Greater than or equal to |
| <> | Not equal to |

# Operation Extenders

You use operation extenders with operation codes to specify an option. The operation extenders that are available vary by operation code, and, if used, must be entered immediately after an operation code within parentheses. No blank space is permitted between the operation code and the extender. More than one operation extender is available for some operations.

| Operation extender | Description |
|---|---|
| a | Used on the Dump operation to override Debug(*No) specified on the H control specification |
| e | Enable error handling with the %Error built-in function |
| h | Half adjust (round) a numeric operation |
| m | Use default precision rules |
| n | For a record read, do not lock |
| n | For a Dealloc operation, set pointer to *Null |
| p | Pad resulting character string with blanks |
| d | On a bound call, pass operational descriptors |
| d | On a Test operation, designates test for date |
| r | Use result decimal precision rules |
| t | On a Test operation, test for time |
| z | On a Test operation, test for timestamp |

# Free-Format Operations

The following operations are permitted in free-format RPG IV.

### ACQ (Acquire)

Acq{(e)} *device-name workstation-file-name*

The Acq operation acquires the program device specified by the *device-name* parameter that has been specified within the multiple-device file specified by the *workstation-file-name* parameter. This file is probably an Intersystem Communications Facility (ICF) file that uses Workstn as its device on file specifications.

```
Example:
Acq Eudev1 RemotesysF;
```

## BEGSR (Beginning of subroutine)

BegSr *subroutine-name*

The BegSr operation specifies the beginning of a subroutine. You code subroutines after the main procedure and use operation code ExSr (Invoke subroutine) to perform them. The special subroutines *INZSR and *PSSR are invoked according to special rules. A subroutine might also be invoked automatically if it is named as a parameter of the file keyword INFSR (information subroutine). The EndSr (End subroutine) operation marks the end of a subroutine.

```
Example:
Begsr AddRecord;
```

## CALLP (Call a prototyped procedure or program)

CallP{(emr)} *name({parm1:parm2:...})*

The CallP operation is used to call a prototyped procedure or program specified by the operation's *name* parameter. Parameters to pass to the program or procedure are specified in a list within parentheses, using a colon (:) between parameters. The parameter list must match the prototype. You can specify up to 399 parameters when calling a procedure or up to 255 parameters when calling a program. If operation extenders are not required, the CallP operation code itself may be omitted. If a subprocedure is being called and the subprocedure has a return value, the procedure call can be specified within an evaluation expression or a comparison expression.

```
Examples:
CallP FileUpd(CustName:OrderNum); // Explicit call

Total_Tax = Compute_tax(Marital:Taxable_Amt:Exem) +
            Extra_Tax;            // Implicit call
```

## CHAIN (Random retrieval from a file)

Chain{(en)} *search-argument name {data-structure}*

The Chain operation attempts to retrieve a record directly from a full procedural file. The *search-argument* parameter can be a key (or a list of keys) if the file description for the file specifies K for record address type. The search argument can also be a relative record number. The *name* parameter can be a file name or a file's record format name. If you use the optional *data-structure* parameter, the record data is placed into the specified data structure. If no data structure is specified, data for the record is placed into the field definitions for the file. You can use the %Found built-in function after the Chain operation to determine the success of the retrieval.

```
Example:
Chain (Custnum:order_num) Orderfile;
```

## CLEAR (Clear)

Clear {*Nokey} {*All} *name*

The Clear operation sets the named item to the default initialization value for the data type(s) involved. The *name* parameter names a record format, data structure, array, table, field, data structure subfield, array element, or indicator. Character data types are set to blanks; numeric data types are set to 0 (zero). The *Nokey option is used with data files. If you specify *Nokey with a data file record format, all fields in the record except the key fields are cleared. The *All option is used with multiple-occurrence data structures and tables. If you specify *All, the Clear operation clears all occurrences or all table entries. If *All is not specified, the operation clears only the current occurrence or current table entry.

```
Example:
Clear ScreenRec;
```

## CLOSE (Close files)

Close{(e)} *file-name* -or- *All

The Close operation either closes the specified file or, if the *All option is specified, closes all currently open files. The file cannot be a table file. If the file specified on the Close is already closed, no error occurs.

```
Example:
Close  ArMaster;
```

## COMMIT (Commit)

Commit{(e)} {*boundary*}

The Commit operation makes all file changes that have been performed since the last Commit or Rollback operation and releases all the record locks for files under commitment control. The *boundary* option is a constant or non-pointer variable used to identify the changes made by the Commit.

```
Example:
Commit;
```

## DEALLOC (Free storage)

Dealloc{(en)} *pointer-name*

The Deallocate operation causes storage previously allocated in a dynamic heap to be freed. The *pointer-name* parameter is required; it refers to the pointer used by a previous Alloc (Allocate storage) or Realloc (Reallocate storage) operation. Dynamic storage APIs can also set the pointer. If you specify the operation extender (n), the pointer is set to *Null after a successful deallocation.

```
Example:
Dealloc array_ptr;
```

## DELETE (Delete record)

Delete{(ehmr)} {*search-argument*} *name*

The Delete operation tries to delete a record from a database file. The file must have U (for Update) specified as the file type. If no *search-argument* value is specified, the last record read (via any Read operation or a Chain operation) is deleted from the file. If a search argument is specified, it must be a key, a list of keys, or a relative record number. The key or list of keys is used to locate the record if the file specified K in the record address type. Relative record number can be used for non-keyed files. If no record exists in the data file that matches the key, no record is deleted.

You can use built-in function %Found after the Delete to determine whether a record was found (and deleted) or not found. The *name* parameter specifies a file name or a record format name of a database file.

```
Example:
Delete OrderRec;
```

## DOU (Do until)

Dou{(mr)} *expression*

The Dou operation begins a group of operations (ended by an Enddo operation) that is to be performed at least once and possibly many times. The expression can be an indicator or a test-type expression, such as Fld1>Fld2. The test for true will be made at the Enddo. If the indicator is on or the expression is true, control is set to the next instruction after the Enddo. If the indicator is off or the expression is false, control is returned to the beginning of the Dou group. You can specify a compound expression on the Dou operation.

```
Example:
Dou exit or Error_code > *zero;
```

## DOW (Do while)

Dow{(mr)} *expression*

The Dow operation begins a group of operations (ended by an Enddo operation). Depending on the truth of the expression, the group of operations may or may not be performed, even once. The expression can be an indicator or a test-type expression, such as Fld1>Fld2. The test for true is made at the Dow operation. If the indicator is on or the expression is true, control is set to the next operation after the Dow. If the indicator is off or the expression is false, control is set to the operation following the Enddo operation that concludes the Dow. You can use a compound expression on the Dow operation.

```
Example:
Dow Not %eof and Error_code <> 105;
```

## DSPLY (Display message)

Dsply{(e)} {*M *message-id* -or- *field* {*message-queue* {*response*}}}

The Dsply operation is used to communicate to and possibly from the display workstation that requested this program. This operation has many possible options. If *M and a *message-id* value are specified, the *message-id* is located in message file QUSERMSG. If a *field* value (which also may be a constant) is used, the contents are sent to the user. The *message-queue* parameter is optional; it defaults to the job external message queue. You can specify other message queues as constants or as variable names. If information is to be returned to the program, you must specify a *response* parameter. The operation places the information provided by the workstation user into the *response* field.

```
Example:
Dsply 'What is your name?' '' Name;
```

## DUMP (Program dump)

Dump{(a)} {*identifier*}

The Dump operation provides the ability to print a listing of the contents of all fields, file information, indicators, data structures, arrays, and tables used by the program. If the compiler parameter DbgView(*None) is specified, only the contents of the program status data structure, file information data structures, and numbered indicators are listed. If the H control specification specifies Debug(*No), no dump will be performed unless you specify the operation extender (a). The Dump operation places the contents of the constant or variable *identifier* in the heading of the listing.

```
Example:
Dump 'Point_A';
```

## ELSE (Else)

Else

The Else operation is an option in a control-logic If group. If the test expression used on the If or subsequent Elseifs is not true, the operations following the Else are performed, up to the required Endif. If the test expression on the If or any subsequent Elseif is true, the operations after the Else are not performed.

```
Example:
Else;
```

## ELSEIF (Else if)

Elseif{(mr)} *test-expression*

The Elseif operation is a combination of an Else and an If. Using this operation requires fewer levels of If nesting. You place the Elseif within a control-logic If group. If the test expression of the If is not true, control is passed to the Elseif. The test expression of the Elseif is then checked. If the expression is true, the operations following the Elseif are performed, up to the next Elseif, Else, or Endif operations.

```
Example:
Elseif Amount > 100.00;
```

## ENDDO (End a Dou or Dow group)

Enddo

The Enddo operation ends a Dou (Do until) or Dow (Do while) logic structure. For details about these group operations, see the descriptions of the Dou and Dow operations elsewhere in this appendix.

```
Example:
Enddo;
```

## ENDFOR (End a For group)

Endfor

The Endfor operation ends a For logic structure. For details about this group operation, see the description of the For operation.

```
Example:
Endfor;
```

## ENDIF (End an If group)

Endif

The Endif operation ends an If logic structure. See the If, Elseif, and Else operation descriptions for details about these group operations.

```
Example:
Endif;
```

## ENDMON (End a Monitor group)

Endmon

The Endmon operation ends a Monitor group. See the Monitor and On-Error operation descriptions for details about these group operations.

```
Example:
Endmon;
```

## ENDSL (End a Select group)

Endsl

The Endsl operation ends a Select group. See the Select, When, and Other operation descriptions for details about these group operations.

```
Example:
Endsl;
```

## ENDSR (End subroutine)

Endsr *return-point*

The EndSr operation is the termination operation for a subroutine. When this operation is performed, control in the program resumes at the operation after the Exsr operation that requested the subroutine.

Some exceptions exist. For the *INZSR subroutine, control is passed to the first operation of the main procedure. For the *PSSR subroutine or file exception subroutines (value specified on file keyword INFSR), you can specify the *return-point* parameter. Program cycle options are available, but the most likely value of *return-point* is either '*CANCL' or a field containing blanks.

```
Example:
Endsr;
```

## EVAL (Evaluate expression)

{Eval{(hmr)}} *result operator expression*

The Eval (evaluation) operation performs the functions specified in the *expression* parameter and places the results into the *result* field according to the dictates of the specified *operator*. The operator is most likely the = (assignment) operator, but the accumulation operators +=, -=, *=, and /= are possible. If no operation extenders are needed, you can omit the operation code (Eval).

The data type of the expression to be evaluated must be the same as the data type of the result variable. For character expressions, the result of the expression is left-justified in the result variable, and the result field is padded with blanks (to the right).

```
Examples:
Eval(h) Newrate *= .005;

Line_4 = %trim(city)+ ', ' + State + '  ' + Zip;
```

## EVAL-CORR (Move to corresponding subfields)

Eval-Corr{(hmr)} *target = source*

The Eval-Corr operation moves data and null indicators from a source data structure to a target data structure. This is a "smart" move in that the move matches on subfield name and compatible data type rather than location. The optional (h) operation code extender will half adjust numeric fields as they are moved. Because this operation uses the subfield name to match, either the source or the target, or both data structures, must be qualified.

If both data structures are defined like the same data structure, the data structure is moved as a whole, rather than by subfield name.

```
Example:
Eval-Corr TargetDS = SourceDS;
```

## EVALR (Evaluate expression, right adjust)

EvalR{(mr)} *result = expression*

The EvalR operation performs the functions specified in the *expression* parameter and places the results in the *result* field. Only the = assignment operator is permitted. The final results of the expression must be of type character, graphic, or UCS-2, which means that the result variable must be the same. The expression's result is right-justified in the result variable, and the result field is padded with blanks (to the left).

```
Example:
Evalr Message = 'Operation complete';
```

*Note:* In this example, if Message is defined as character with length 20, the value of Message is ' Operation complete' after the instruction is executed.

## EXCEPT (Calculation time output)

Except {*exception-name*}

The Except operation lets you perform program-described record output immediately. Output to be performed must be described in output specifications.
Output records must have an output type of E and a name that matches the
*exception-name* value specified on the Except operation. Multiple output records
can be described using the same *exception-name* value. The output is performed
in the order of the output specifications. If no *exception-name* value is specified,
records in output with no name are written.

```
Example:
Except Print_Line;
```

## EXFMT (Write/then read format)

Exfmt{(e)} *record-format-name*

The Exfmt operation is a combination of a "write record" operation followed
immediately by a "read record" operation. The operation works only on files with
device Workstn specified. You can use display files or ICF files if they are
described as full procedural, externally described, and file type combined.

The *record-format-name* value must be the same as a record name in the
workstation file. The Exfmt operation causes the program to stop and wait for
input from the device. The wait time is indefinitely long.

```
Example:
Exfmt Dspfcontrl;
```

## EXSR (Invoke subroutine)

ExSr *subroutine-name*

The ExSr operation moves program control to the subroutine specified as *subroutine-name*. At the conclusion of the subroutine, control is passed to the operation following the ExSr operation. The *subroutine-name* value must match the *subroutine-name* value specified on a BegSr operation, anywhere in the program. *Note:* All subroutines must be placed after the main procedure.

```
Example:
ExSr Add_record;
```

## FEOD (Force end of data)

Feod{(en)} *file-name*

The Feod operation sets the file specified in the *file-name* parameter to logical end-of-data. The Feod function differs depending on the file type and device. Feod does not close the file, but to re-access sequential data in a file, you must either use a Setgt or Setll instruction (before a Read or ReadP) or use a Chain operation.

```
Example:
Feod FileA;
```

## FOR (For)

For{(mr)} *index-name* {=*start-value*} {BY *increment-value*} {TO -or-
DOWNTO *limit-value*}

The For operation begins a group of operations, the end of which is indicated by
an Endfor operation. The *index-name* value determines the number of times the
group is repeated. The optional parameters *start-value, increment-value,* and
*limit-value* can be numeric constants, fields, or expressions with zero decimal
positions. If no start value is specified, the *index-name* variable starts with
whatever value it had before the For group. If the {BY *increment-value*} option is
not specified, the index increment is 1 (one). If the {TO -or- DOWNTO *limit-value*}
option is not specified, the For group will repeat either indefinitely or until a loop
interrupter operation (e.g., Leave) is performed.

The For group is normally ended when the *index-name* value is greater than
the limit (for the TO limit option) or less than the limit (for the DOWNTO option).

```
Examples:
For index = 1 To %elem(Array);

For I = %len(FieldA) Downto 1;
```

## FORCE (Force a certain file to be read next cycle)

Force *file-name*

The Force operation is used when the RPG cycle and both primary and secondary
files are specified. You must specify Force at detail time. The *file-name* value
causes the next record read to come from the named file, altering the normal
multifile processing scheme of the cycle.

```
Example:
Force Orderfile;
```

## IF (If)

If{(mr)} *test-expression*

The If operation begins a group of operations ended by an Endif operation. The operations specified after the If are performed if the test expression resolves to true. The test expression can be an indicator (*On = true, *Off = false), a relationship expression, and combinations using And and Or. The Elseif and Else operations may optionally appear in an If group.

```
Example:
If FieldA > FieldB Or Arry(I) = 75.00;
```

## IN (Retrieve a data area)

In{(e)} {*Lock} *data-area-name*

You use the In operation to retrieve the contents of a data area and place them in a program variable or data structure. The *Lock option is available to prevent other programs from updating the data area after the current program retrieves it—similar in concept to a record lock in a database file. You cannot use the *Lock option if the data area is the local data area or the program initialization parameter data area.

The *data-area-name* value matches the value used in the DTAARA keyword of a definition specification, the result field (fixed-format style) of a Define operation that uses the *DTAARA option in Factor 1, or the special value *DTAARA. If you use the *DTAARA value on an In operation, the operation retrieves all data areas defined in the program. If one or more of the data areas cannot be retrieved (because of the *Lock option), an error occurs. To write to a data area, use the Out operation.

```
Example:
In *Lock StartVals;
```

## ITER (Iterate)

Iter

The Iter operation is used within a Dou, Dow, or For block to have the program transfer control to the Enddo or Endfor of the group. The next iteration of the group will be then performed. If the Enddo is for a Dou, the test condition is performed to determine whether to repeat the group or leave the group.

```
Example:
Dou Exit;
  Exfmt Edit;
  If cust_name = *Blank;
    Err_name = *On;
    Iter;
  Endif;
    .
    .
    .
Enddo;
```

## LEAVE (Leave a Do/For group)

Leave

The Leave operation is used to exit a Dou, Dow, or For group. When performed, the Leave transfers control to the next operation after the innermost Do or For group. In nested Do or For groups, the Leave operation moves outward only one level.

```
Example:
For I = 1 to 10;
  Read FileA;
  If %eof(FileA);
    Leave;
  Endif;
Endfor;
```

## LEAVESR (Leave a subroutine)

LeaveSr

You use the LeaveSr operation within a subroutine to exit the subroutine from any point.

```
Example:
Begsr Check_order;
Chain key Order_file;
If not %found(Order_file);
  Err_not_found = *on;
  LeaveSr;
Endif;
.
.
.
Endsr;
```

## MONITOR (Begin a Monitor group)

Monitor

The Monitor operation begins a group of operations that are to be checked for errors. Many operations (e.g., Eval) don't have the (e) error operation extender option. You can use a Monitor group to check for and handle exceptions occurring between the Monitor operation and the first On-error statement. The checking and handling are specified by an On-error operation and statements following it. For more details about this function, see the description of the On-error operation.

An Endmon operation concludes a Monitor group. If no errors occur during execution of a Monitor group, control is passed to the next operation after the Endmon statement. If a Monitor group is nested within another Monitor group, the inner Monitor is handled first. If the inner Monitor doesn't handle the exception, the outer Monitor is used.

```
Example:
Monitor;
  A = B*C/D;
  On-error;
    // Handle error here
Endmon;
```

## NEXT (Next)

Next{(e)} *program-device file-name*

The Next operation tells the multiple-device *file-name* which *program-device* to use for the next input function, assuming that the input method is the program cycle read or a read-by-file. Program device names are specified in multiple-device files, such as ICF files.

```
Example:
Next Cash_Reg_27 Icffile;
```

## ON-ERROR (On error)

On-error {*exception-code* {*exception-code* ...}}

You use the On-error operation within a Monitor group. The *exception-code* value(s) can be one of the special values *Program, *File, or *All or a five-digit program or status code. If you specify no exception code, the *All option is used. If you specify the *Program option, status values from 100 to 999 are checked. If you specify *File, status values from 1000 to 9999 are checked. Status values below 100 cannot be monitored. You can also specify specific status codes, separated by blanks. If any of the status codes checked are true, the operations after On-error are performed, up to the next On-error or Endmon statement.

```
Example:
Monitor;
 Read File_A;
 A = B/G;
  On-error *File;
     // Handle file errors here
  On-error *ALL;
     // Handle math errors here
Endmon;
```

## OPEN (Open file for processing)

Open{(e)} *file-name*

The Open operation is used when the file named in the *file-name* parameter used the UsrOpn keyword on the file description. When the UsrOpn keyword is not used, the file is opened at program initialization. You can use the Open operation more than once in a program if the file is closed (Close operation). If you use Open on a file that is already open, an error occurs. You can test to see whether a file is open by using the built-in function %Open.

```
Example:
Open(e) Printfile;
```

## OTHER (Otherwise select)

Other

You specify the Other operation within a Select group after all When operations. The Other operation is optional within the group and begins a group of operations to be performed if none of the When conditions is true. You can specify only one Other operation for a Select group.

```
Example:
Select;
  When Option = A;
    Exsr  Add_Rec_Subr;
  When Option = C;
    Exsr Change_Rec_Subr;
  Other;
    Errmsg = 'Invalid option entered';
    Option_Err = *ON;
Endsl;
```

## OUT (Write a data area)

Out{(e)} {* Lock} *data-area-name*

You use the Out operation to update the data area named by the *data-area-name* parameter. The *data-area-name* value must match the value of the DTAARA keyword used on definition specifications or the result field (fixed-format style) of a Define operation that uses the *DTAARA value in Factor 1. The data area must have been previously locked by the *Lock option of an In operation, or it must be connected to a data-area data structure with U specified as the data structure type. The *Lock option on the Out operation causes the data area to remain locked after the update. Without this option, the data area is unlocked after the Out operation.

```
Example:
OUT StartVals;
```

## POST (Post)

POST{(e)} {*program-device*} *file-name*

The Post operation lets you place feedback information into a file's information data structure. The *program-device* parameter is used only for multiple-device files, to place specific information about the specified device into the data structure. The file information data structure is normally updated after any input or output operation to the file. If a Post operation with no program device is specified in a program, only portions of the file information data structure are updated when the Post is encountered.

```
Example:
Post Cash_Reg_27 ICF_file;
```

## READ (Read a record)

Read{(en)} *name* {*data-structure*}

The Read operation is used on a full procedural file to obtain the next record at the current location of the file pointer. The *name* parameter is required and must be a file name or a record format name. If the operation is successful, the record data is set to the new values, and the file pointer is positioned to the next record. If an error occurs or end-of-file is reached, the record data is not changed. If you use the *data-structure* parameter, the operation moves the record data into the specified data structure. For externally described files, the data structure must be defined with either the ExtName(*file-name*:*Input) keyword and option or the LikeRec(*record-name*:*Input) keyword and option.

```
Example:
Read DBFile;
```

## READC (Read next changed record)

ReadC{(e)} *record-name* {*data-structure*}

The ReadC operation is available only for files using device Workstn. It is used to retrieve the next changed record in a display file's subfile. The *record-name* value must be the name of a record format defined as a subfile record on the file description's Sfile keyword. If no more changed records exist in the subfile, no data is returned, and the %Eof (end-of-file) test will return *On. If you specify the *data-structure* parameter, the operation moves the record data into the specified data structure. The data structure must be defined with the ExtName(*file-name*:*Input) or LikeRec(*record-name*:*Input) keyword and option.

```
Example:
Dou %eof;
  ReadC SubfRec;
  If not %eof;
     // Process subfile record
  Endif;
Enddo;
```

## READE (Read equal key)

ReadE{(enhmp)} *search-argument name {data-structure}*

The ReadE operation attempts to read the next record from the location of the current file pointer. The *search-argument* parameter is required; it determines whether a record is read or an end-of-file condition is set. If the *search-argument* value matches the key of the record, the data is read, and the file pointer is moved to the next record. If the *search-argument* value does not match the key of the record, no data is read, and the EOF condition is set. The search argument can be a single field, a literal, a named constant, or a figurative constant. It can also be the name of a Klist (fixed-format style) or a list of values within parentheses separated by colons (:). You can also use the %Kds built-in function, with subfields from a data structure defined using the LikeRec(*record-name*:*Key) keyword and option.

The *search-argument* value can also be *Key. In this case, if the entire key of the next record matches the key of the last record read, the next record is retrieved. The *name* parameter must be the name of a file or a record format. If you specify the *data-structure* parameter, the operation moves the record data into the specified data structure. The data structure must be defined with the ExtName(*file-name*:*Input) or LikeRec(*record-name*:*Input) keyword and option. If a ReadE operation sets the end-of-file condition, the file pointer must be reset using a Set type operation or a Chain operation.

```
Example:
ReadE (Company_No:Customer_No) Invoice;
```

## READP (Read prior record)

ReadP{(en)} *name {data-structure}*

The ReadP operation attempts to read the previous record from a full procedural file at the current location of the file pointer. The *name* parameter is required; it must be the name of a file or record format to be read. If the ReadP is successful, the record data is changed to the new values, and the file pointer is positioned to the previous record. If an error occurs or beginning-of-file is reached, the record data is not changed. If beginning-of-file is reached, the EOF condition is set. You can check this condition using the %Eof built-in function. If you specify the *data-structure* parameter, the operation moves the record data into the specified data structure. For externally described files, the data structure must be defined with the ExtName(*file-name*:*Input) or LikeRec(*record-name*:*Input) keyword and option.

```
Example:
ReadP DBFile;
```

## READPE (Read prior equal)

ReadPE{(enhmr)} *search-argument name*

The ReadPE operation works the same as the ReadE operation, but it checks and retrieves the previous record rather than the next record. For details, see the description of ReadE.

```
Example:
ReadPE (customer_no:invno) Transact;
```

## REL (Release)

Rel{(e)} *program-device file-name*

The Rel operation releases the program device (*program-device*) specified in the multiple-device file named in the *file-name* parameter. No further requests can be made for this program device after a successful Rel.

```
Example:
Rel Eurdev_1 Remotesysf;
```

## RESET (Reset)

Reset{(e)} {*Nokey} {*All} *name*

The Reset operation is used to set one or more variables to the values they had at the end of the initialization phase of program startup. If there is no *INZSR subroutine, the reset values are the initialize values. If no INZ keyword is used on the variables, numeric variables are initialized to 0 (zero), and character variables are initialized to blanks. If an *INZSR subroutine is used, the reset values of variables are determined at the conclusion of the *INZSR subroutine. You use the *Nokey option on database record formats to reset all variables in the record except the key fields.

You use the *All option with multiple-occurrence data structures, tables, and a format record. If *All is specified, all occurrences, table entries, and record fields are reset. If *All is not specified, only the current occurrence or table entry is reset. If *All is not used in a record format, only fields designated for output are reset. The *name* parameter specifies a field, record format, data structure, array, or table.

```
Example:
Reset *All RecFile8;
```

## RETURN (Return to caller)

Return{(hmr)} *expression*

The Return operation is used to return control to the calling program. You use the *expression* parameter with a subprocedure Return when a return value has been defined in the prototype of the subprocedure. If a main procedure performs a Return operation, the setting of the *Inlr indicator is significant. If *Inlr is set on before the Return, program files are closed, data areas are unlocked and written, array and table data is written, and the program ends normally. If *Inlr is set off before the Return operation, files are not closed, no action is taken with data areas, tables, and arrays, and the program's variables are left in static storage with current values. A subsequent call to the program will not initialize variables or run the *INZSR subroutine.

```
Example (in a subprocedure):
Return(h) Field_4 * Field_5;
```

## ROLBK (Roll back)

RolBk{(e)}

The Rolbk operation performs the following actions:

- Removes all changes made to files since the last Commit or RolBk operation or since the start of commitment control
- Releases any record locks for files under commitment control
- Sets the file pointer to its position at the time of the last commit or to beginning-of-file (if no previous commit has run)

```
Example:
Rolbk;
```

## SELECT (Begin a Select group)

Select

The Select operation begins a group of operations that includes the When operation and an optional Other operation. The When operation tests for a condition and, if true, permits operations specified after the When to run, up to the next When (or Other). Program control then resumes at the operation following the EndSl (End select). You can specify additional When specifications after the first, and so on, with the Other operation and the statements following it covering the logical possibility that none of the previous conditions is true.

A Select group provides a structured way to check the value of a user option and perform the correct operations based on the option's value. A Select group ends with an EndSl operation.

```
Example:
Select;
  When Option = A;
    Exsr  Add_Rec_Subr;
  When Option = C;
    Exsr Change_Rec_Subr;
  Other;
    Errmsg = 'Invalid option entered';
    Option_Err = *On;
EndSl;
```

## SETGT (Set greater than)

Setgt{(ehmr)} *search-argument record-name* -or- *file-name*

You use the Setgt operation with a full procedural database file to set the position of the file pointer. The file pointer is set to the record whose key or relative record number is greater than (but closest to) the key or relative record number specified in the *search-argument* parameter. If a key is being used, the search argument can be a single key value or a series of key values separated by colons. It can also be the name of a Klist (fixed-format style) or the built-in function %Kds specified with the name of a data structure defined using the LikeRec(*record-name*:*Key) keyword and options. To determine whether a qualifying record exists in the file, use the %Found built-in function after the Setgt operation. A Read or ReadE operation usually follows a Setgt operation.

```
Example:
Setgt (comp_no:cust_num) transactn;
```

## SETLL (Set lower limit)

Setll{(ehmr)} *search-argument record-name* -or- *file-name*

You use the Setll operation with a full procedural database file to set the position of the file pointer. The file pointer is set to the record whose key or relative record number is equal to or greater than the *search-argument* value. If a key is being used, the search argument can be a single key value or a series of key values separated by colons. It can also be the name of a Klist (fixed-format style) or the built-in function %Kds specified with the name of a data structure defined using the LikeRec(*record name*:*Key) keyword and options. Use the %Found built-in function after the Setll operation to determine whether a record exists. You can also use the %Equal function after the Setll operation to determine whether an exact match was found. A Read or ReadE operation usually follows a Setll operation.

```
Example:
Setll (Cust_No:Order_Num) CustOrders;
```

## SORTA (Sort an array)

SortA *array-name*

-or-

SortA %Subarr(*array:start-elem* {*num-elems*})

The SortA operation lets you sort elements of an array into ascending or descending sequence based on the keyword specified for the array on the definition specifications. If the array definition specifies no sequence, ascending sequence is used. The indicator array *In cannot be sorted. If the array uses the Overlay keyword, the SortA operation sorts the base array using the sequence defined by the Overlay array.

```
Example:
SortA Array3;
```

## TEST (Test date/time/timestamp)

Test{(edtz)} {*format*} *field-name*

The Test operation lets you test a numeric or character field to see whether the field contains a valid date, time, or timestamp, depending on the *format* you specify. To check for errors, you must include the (e) operation extender. If an error is determined, the %Error built-in function can check for it after the Test operation. The Test operation can also check a date, time, or timestamp data type field. In this case, you omit the *format* parameter.

```
Example:
Dcl-S  Cdate Char(6) Inz('0916604');
Test(e) *MDYO Cdate;
```

*Note:* In this example, no error occurs on the operation because Cdate is a valid date that matches the format specified.

## UNLOCK (Unlock a data area or release a record)

Unlock{(e)} *name* -or- *DTAARA

The Unlock operation is used to unlock the named data area or unlock a record in a file that was locked with a Read or Chain (file type Update). Unlocking the record may prevent a record lock condition. If the *name* parameter specifies a data area, the name must also be specified in the DTAARA keyword of a definition specification or in the result field of a Define (fixed-format style) operation that specifies * DTAARA in Factor 1. If the parameter of the Unlock operation is the special value *DTAARA, all data areas in the program that are locked are unlocked.

```
Data Area Example:
Unlock Startda;        // One data area
Unlock *DTAARA;        // All data areas

Record Example:
Unlock UpdFileR;       // Unlock record just read
```

## UPDATE (Modify existing record)

Update{(e)} *name* {*data-structure* -or- %Fields(*name*{:*name*...})}

The Update operation is used to modify the record just read for update (via a Read or Chain operation) and locked. The *name* parameter can be a file name or a record format name. For externally described files, the name must be a record format name. No operation can be performed on the file from the Read or Chain (with lock) and the Update operation. If you use the *data-structure* option, the record is updated from data in the data structure. If you update using this method and the file is externally described, the data structure must be defined with the ExtName(*file-name*:*Input) or LikeRec(*record-name*:*Input) keyword and option. If you update using the %Fields built-in function option, the field names must match the field names of the record format. The number of fields supplied can be a subset of the total number specified in the record. Without the %Fields option, the operation updates all fields of the record.

```
Example:
Update DBrecord %fields(Name:zip);
```

## WHEN (When true then select)

When{(mr)} *test-expression*

The When operation is used within a Select group to test an indicator, a logical expression, or both. If the indicator is on or the test expression is true, the operations following the When are performed, up to the next When, Other, or Endsl operation. Compound expressions are permitted (using And and Or). See the descriptions of the Select and Other operations for more information about these operations.

```
Example:
Select;
  When Option = A;
    Exsr  Add_Rec_Subr;
  When Option = C;
    Exsr Change_Rec_Subr;
  Other;
    Errmsg = 'Invalid option entered';
    Option_Err = *On;
Endsl;
```

## WRITE (Create new records)

Write{(e)} *name {data-structure}*

A Write operation creates a new record in a file. The *name* parameter must be the name of a file or record format. For a program-described file, a file name is used; for an externally described file, a record format name is used. If you use the *data-structure* option, the Write uses the data from the data structure to write the new record. If an externally described file is used, the data structure must be defined with the ExtName(*file-name*:*Output) or LikeRec(*record-name*:*Output) keyword and option. When you use Write to add records to a database file, the file must have O (letter O) as the file type or A specified as the file addition option.

```
Example:
Write RecName;
```

## XML-INTO (Parse an XML document into a variable)

Xml-Into *variable* %XML(*xmldoc{:options}*)

-or-

Xml-Into %Handler(*handler-proc*:*Commarea*) %Xml(*xmldoc{:options}*)

Xml-Into can operate in either of these two formats. The first syntax moves XML data directly into the variable. The second syntax moves data into an array parameter that is then passed to the procedure that is specified by the *handler-proc* parameter.

The first operand (in either format) is the receiver of the XML data. The second operand must be the %Xml built-in-function specifying the XML document. The *options* parameter control the way parsing is done. For details about the available options, see the documentation for the %Xml built-in function.

The IBM manual *Rational Development Studio for i ILE RPG Language Reference* (SC09-2508) includes many pages of examples of the XML-INTO operation.

```
Example:
XML-INTO  data  %xml('data.xml':'doc=file');
```

## XML-SAX (Parse an XML document)

XML-SAX{(e)} %Handler(*handler-proc*:*Commarea*) %Xml(*xmldoc*{:*options*})

XML-SAX parses an XML document, as does XML-INTO. However, XML-SAX offers more control and flexibility than XML-INTO does. In case you are wondering, SAX stands for <u>S</u>imple <u>A</u>PI for <u>X</u>ML. The XML-SAX operation starts an XML parse. When the parser finds the beginning of an event ('<'), it calls the *handler-proc* procedure with the parameters that describe the event. When the handler is done, the parser keeps going until it finds another event ('<'); then it calls the handler again. After all events are parsed, control passes to the next operation after the XML-SAX.

The second parameter of the XML-SAX operation defines the XML document to be parsed using the %Xml built-in function. For details about the available options, see the documentation for the %Xml built-in function.

IBM's *Rational Development Studio for i ILE RPG Language Reference* (SC09-2508) provides many pages of examples of the XML-SAX operation.

```
Example:
XML-SAX &Handler(Handler:CommArea) %xml('jim/myxml.xml':
                                         'doc=file');
```

# B

# Example Screens, DDS, and Programs

This appendix provides the complete listings (sample screens, DDS, and programs) for the four sample free-format RPG IV programs presented in Chapter 12: the investment and loan utility, the customer inquiry program, the customer data entry application, and the sales report program.

## Investment and Loan Utility Program

Listing B-1 shows the screen for the investment and loan utility program. Listing B-2 shows the DDS for the screen. Listing B-3 shows the RPG IV program.

Listing B-4 shows the display after some data has been entered. From this sample display, we can discern the following information:

- The user invests a lump sum of $1,000 now at a 3 percent annual rate of interest. The user also puts $100 into the account each period, starting now. The total amount saved after 120 periods (10 years) is $15,323.49.

- The user borrows $200,000 at 6.5 percent interest annually and wants to know the principal and interest payment if the loan is for 360 periods (30 years). The payment is $1,264.66, and if payments are made over the entire 30 years, the total paid out is $455,277.60.

```
A100XXXC                 Investment and Loan Utility              3/14/15
JIM                                                               14:35:42

                         Investment Computations

              Initial Investment Amount:      _____
           Annual interest rate (decimal):    .00000
                      Number of periods:      __0
           Investment amount each period:     _____

     Value of Investment at the conclusion:              .00

                          Loan Computations

                      Amount to Borrow:       _____
           Annual interest rate (decimal):    .00000
                      Number of periods:      ___
           *OR*       Payment Amount:         _____
                      Total of Payments:               .00



     F3 = Exit      Enter to run
```

Listing B-1: Investment and Loan Utility display screen

```
     A                                      DSPSIZ(24 80 *DS3)
     A                                      INDARA
     A          R RIANDL
     A                                      CA03(03 'Exit')
     A                                  1 27'Investment and Loan Utility'
     A                                  1 70DATE
     A                                      EDTCDE(Y)
     A                                  2 70TIME
     A                                  2  3USER
     A                                  1  3SYSNAME
     A                                  4 29'Investment Computations'
     A                                      COLOR(BLU)
     A                                  6 17'Initial Investment Amount:'
     A                                  7 12'Annual interest rate (decimal):'
     A                                  8 25'Number of periods:'
     A                                  9 13'Investment amount each period:'
     A                                 11  5'Value of Investment at the conclus-
     A                                      ion:'
     A                                 13 32'Loan Computations'
     A                                      COLOR(BLU)
     A                                 15 26'Amount to Borrow:'
     A                                 16 12'Annual interest rate (decimal):'
     A                                 17 25'Number of periods:'
     A                                 18 18'*OR*'
     A                                      COLOR(RED)
     A                                 18 28'Payment Amount:'
     A                                 19 25'Total of Payments:'
     A            ERRMSG      60A  O 21 11
     A            INVESTAMT    7Y 2B  6 46EDTCDE(4)
     A            INVANNRATE   5Y 5B  7 46EDTCDE(1)
     A            INVPERIODS   3Y 0B  8 46EDTCDE(1)
```

```
A                INVPERDAMT    6Y 2B  9 46EDTCDE(4)
A                TOTINVEST$   10Y 20 11 46EDTCDE(1)
A                LOANAMOUNT    9Y 2B 15 46EDTCDE(4)
A                LOANANNRAT    5Y 5B 16 46EDTCDE(1)
A                LOANPERIOD    3Y 0B 17 46EDTCDE(4)
A                LOANPAYMNT    8Y 2B 18 46EDTCDE(4)
A                LOANTPAYMT   11Y 20 19 46EDTCDE(1)
A                                    23  7'F3 = Exit'
A                                    23 22'Enter to run'
```

*Listing B-2: DDS for the Investment and Loan Utility screen*

```
Dcl-F IandL workstn indds(inds);

Dcl-ds inds;
  Exit ind pos(3);
End-ds;

Dcl-s Merr ind;
Dcl-s n Packed(4:0);
Dcl-s i Decimal(10:10);
Dcl-s FVsing Packed(11:2);
Dcl-s FVann  Packed(11:2);
Dcl-s PerRate like(InvAnnRate);
Dcl-s ThisPayment like(LoanPaymnt);
Dcl-s RemBalance  like(LoanAmount);
Dcl-s PerInterest Packed(7:2);

Dou exit;                    // Loop until F3
  Exfmt riandl;              //    Bring up screen
  Clear Errmsg;              //    Clear error message
  Clear Merr;                //    Clear error flag
  Clear TotInvest$;          //    Clear investment total

  If not exit;               //    Check for F3 - exit
    If (InvAnnRate > 0 and InvestAmt > 0) or
       (InvAnnRate > 0 and InvPerdAmt > 0); // All fields OK

       n = invperiods;   // Set n - number of periods
       eval(hr) i = InvAnnRate/12;  // Compute monthly rate
       eval(hr) FVsing = InvestAmt * ((1+i) ** n); // FV single
       eval(hr) FVann = InvperdAmt * (((1+i)** n - 1)/i); // Ann
       TotInvest$ = FVsing + FVann; // Sum of single and annuity

    Elseif (InvestAmt > 0 and InvAnnRate = 0) or
           (InvPerdAmt > 0 and InvAnnRate = 0);
       Errmsg = 'Error on Investment parameters'; // Error msg
       Merr = *On;                                // Error flag
    Endif;

    Clear LoanTpaymt;
    Select;
      When LoanPeriod > 0 and LoanAmount > 0 and LoanAnnRat > 0;
        Exsr CalcPayment;
      When LoanPaymnt > 0 and LoanAmount > 0 and LoanAnnRat > 0;
        Exsr CalcNumber;
      Other;
```

*Continued*

```
        If LoanAmount > 0;
           If Merr;
              Errmsg='Errors on both Investment and Loan parameters';
           Else;
              ErrMsg = 'Error on Loan parameters';
           Endif;
        Endif;
   Endsl;

 Endif;
Enddo;
*Inlr = *On;

// Begin subroutines

//   Calculate a loan payment subroutine

Begsr CalcPayment;
Eval(hr) PerRate = LoanAnnRat / 12;       // Get periodic rate
Eval(hr) LoanPaymnt = LoanAmount * (PerRate /
              (1 - ((1.0 + PerRate) ** (LoanPeriod*-1)))));
Eval(h)  LoanTpaymt = LoanPaymnt * LoanPeriod;
Endsr;

//---------------------------------------------------------------

//   Calculate number of payments subroutine

Begsr CalcNumber;
RemBalance = LoanAmount;
Clear LoanTPaymt;
Clear LoanPeriod;
Eval(hr) PerRate = LoanAnnRat / 12;    // Get periodic rate

If LoanPaymnt > 0;
  If RemBalance + (RemBalance * PerRate) - LoanPaymnt
                                   >= RemBalance;
    Errmsg ='Loan payment amount insufficient, please increase amount';
    Leavesr;
  Endif;

  Dou RemBalance = 0;      // Computation loop
    Eval(h)  PerInterest = RemBalance * PerRate;

    If LoanPaymnt <= RemBalance + PerInterest;
      ThisPayment = LoanPaymnt;
      RemBalance  = RemBalance + PerInterest - ThisPayment;

    Else;
      ThisPayment = RemBalance + PerInterest;
      RemBalance  = *zero;
    Endif;

    LoanTpaymt = LoanTpaymt + ThisPayment;
    LoanPeriod = LoanPeriod + 1;

  Enddo;
Endif;
Endsr;
```

Listing B-3: Investment and loan utility RPG IV program

```
A100XXXC                  Investment and Loan Utility              3/14/15
JIM                                                               14:35:42

                          Investment Computations

              Initial Investment Amount:    1000.00
            Annual interest rate (decimal):  .03000
                      Number of periods:    120
            Investment amount each period:   100.00

        Value of Investment at the conclusion:    15,323.49

                          Loan Computations

                      Amount to Borrow:      200000.00
            Annual interest rate (decimal):   .06500
                      Number of periods:     360
              *OR*      Payment Amount:       1264.66
                      Total of Payments:     455,277.60


          F3 = Exit       Enter to run
```

Listing B-4: Investment and Loan Utility display with data entered

# Customer Inquiry Program

Listing B-5 shows the starting display screen for the customer inquiry program.
Listing B-6 shows the DDS for the display file. Listing B-7 shows the RPG IV
program. After the user enters a valid customer number, the program displays a
screen similar to the one shown in Listing B-8.

```
A100XXXC                      Customer Inquiry                    3/14/15
JIM                                                              14:10:29

              Customer Number: _____






          F3 = Exit      Enter = Run Inquiry
```

Listing B-5: Customer Inquiry display screen

```
A                                        DSPSIZ(24 80 *DS3)
A                                        INDARA
A            R RCUSTINQ
A                                        CA03(03 'Exit')
A                                     1  2SYSNAME
A                                     1 33'Customer Inquiry'
A                                     1 70DATE
A                                        EDTCDE(Y)
A                                     2  2USER
A                                     2 70TIME
A                                     4 18'Customer Number:'
A                                        COLOR(WHT)
A              CUSTNUMDF    7Y 0B     4 36EDTCDE(4)
A                                        COLOR(WHT)
A   50                                6 18'Customer Status:'
A   50        CUSTSTATUSR        O    6 36REFFLD(RCUSTOMER/CUSTSTATUS EDXXXX/-
A                                        CUSTOMERP)
A   50                                7 20'Customer Name:'
A   50        CUSTNAME  R         O    7 36REFFLD(RCUSTOMER/CUSTNAME EDXXXX/CU-
A                                        STOMERP)
A   50                                8 10'Customer Address Line 1:'
A   50        CUSTADR1  R         O    8 36REFFLD(RCUSTOMER/CUSTADR1 EDXXXX/CU-
A                                        STOMERP)
A   50                                9 10'Customer Address Line 2:'
A   50        CUSTADR2  R         O    9 36REFFLD(RCUSTOMER/CUSTADR2 EDXXXX/CU-
A                                        STOMERP)
A   50                               10 20'Customer City:'
A   50        CUSTCITY  R         O   10 36REFFLD(RCUSTOMER/CUSTCITY EDXXXX/CU-
A                                        STOMERP)
A   50                               11 19'Customer State:'
A   50        CUSTSTATE R         O   11 36REFFLD(RCUSTOMER/CUSTSTATE EDXXXX/C-
A                                        USTOMERP)
A   50                               12 16'Customer Zip Code:'
A   50        CUSTZIP   R         O   12 36REFFLD(RCUSTOMER/CUSTZIP EDXXXX/CUS-
A                                        TOMERP)
A   50        CUSTZEXT  R         O   12 42REFFLD(RCUSTOMER/CUSTZEXT EDXXXX/CU-
A                                        STOMERP)
A   50                               13 12'Customer Phone Number:'
A   50        CUSTAREACDR        O   13 36REFFLD(RCUSTOMER/CUSTAREACD EDXXXX/-
A                                        CUSTOMERP)
A   50        CUSTPHONE R         O   13 40REFFLD(RCUSTOMER/CUSTPHONE EDXXXX/C-
A                                        USTOMERP)
A   50                               15 14'Customer Amount Due:'
A   50        CUSTAMTDUER        O   15 36REFFLD(RCUSTOMER/CUSTAMTDUE EDXXXX/-
A                                        CUSTOMERP)
A                                        EDTCDE(J)
A   50                               16 12'Customer Credit Limit:'
A   50        CUSTCRLIMTR        O   16 36REFFLD(RCUSTOMER/CUSTCRLIMT EDXXXX/-
A                                        CUSTOMERP)
A                                        EDTCDE(J)
A   50                               18 14'Date Customer Began:'
A   50        DATEOUT      10A   O  18 36
A            ERRMSG       60A   O  21 11COLOR(PNK)
A                                     23  7'F3 = Exit'
A                                     23 22'Enter = Run Inquiry'
```

Listing B-6: DDS for the customer inquiry display file

```
Ctl-Opt option(*srcstmt);
Dcl-F Custinqdf workstn indds(Inds);
Dcl-F CustomerP keyed;

Dcl-DS Inds;
  Exit ind pos(3);
  CustOK ind pos(50);
End-DS;

Dcl-s Date8 packed(8:0);

Dou Exit;                  // Loop until F3 - Exit

  Exfmt RCustInq;          //  Display the screen
  If not exit;
    Clear Errmsg;          // Clear error message
    Clear CustOK;          // Clear indicator
    Chain Custnumdf CustomerP;   // Get customer info
    If %found(CustomerP);      // Check for "found"
      CustOK = *On;            // Set indicator for customer found
      Date8 = CustDatMon * 1000000 + CustDatDay * 10000 + CustDatYr;
      Dateout = %char(%date(Date8:*usa):*usa); // Get date
    Else;
      Errmsg = 'Customer Number entered is invalid, retry.';
    Endif;
  Endif;
Enddo;
*Inlr = *on;
```

*Listing B-7: Customer inquiry RPG IV program*

```
A100XXXC                       Customer Inquiry                    3/14/15
JIM                                                               14:19:16

                 Customer Number:      100

                 Customer Status:  A
                   Customer Name:  ABC Tool Company
         Customer Address Line 1:  1234 Elm Street
         Customer Address Line 2:
                   Customer City:  Chicago
                  Customer State:  IL
               Customer Zip Code:  60606 1313
           Customer Phone Number:  312 555-3567

               Customer Amount Due:  1,342.00
              Customer Credit Limit: 50,000.00

              Date Customer Began:  12/05/2005




      F3 = Exit      Enter = Run Inquiry
```

*Listing B-8: Customer Inquiry results display*

# Customer Data Entry Program

Listing B-9 shows the starting display screen for the customer data entry program. Listing B-10 shows the DDS for the screen. Listing B-11 shows the RPG IV program, and Listing B-12 shows the panel that's displayed if an error is detected as a user enters data. Listings B-13 and B-14 show the two CL programs used by the RPG IV program: CLEARMSG and SENDMSG, respectively. Listing B-15 shows the contents of the message file.

```
A100XXXC                   Customer Data Entry                  3/14/15
JIM                                                            14:21:09

    1 ........             Customer Number:  _____

    2 ........                      Status:  _  (Can only be 'A' or 'I')
    3 ........             Customer Name:     _____
    4 ........             Address Line 1:    _____
    5 ........             Address Line 2:    _____
    6 ........                        City:   _____
    7 ........                       State:   __
    8 ........                    Zip Code:   _____ ____

    9 ........                Credit Limit:   _____.00
   10........            Telephone Number:    _____

   11........                  Begin Date:    __ __ ____  (MM DD YYYY)




        F3 = Exit     F8 = Write new record    Enter = Edit data
```

Listing B-9: Customer Data Entry display

```
A                                    DSPSIZ(24 80 *DS3)
A                                    INDARA
A          R RCSTDATENT
A                                    OVERLAY
A                                    CA03(03 'Exit')
A                                    CF08(08 'Write Record')
A                                  1 2SYSNAME
A                                  1 31'Customer Data Entry'
A                                  1 70DATE
A                                    EDTCDE(Y)
A                                  2 2USER
A                                  2 70TIME
A                                  4 3'1 ............'
A                                  4 23'Customer Number:'
A          CUSTNUM    R    B       4 41REFFLD(RCUSTOMER/CUSTNUMBER -
A                                       CUSTOMERP)
```

```
A                                             EDTCDE(4)
A   41                                         DSPATR(RI PC)
A                                      6  3'2 .............'
A                                      6 32'Status:'
A          CUSTSTAT  R       B   6 41REFFLD(RCUSTOMER/CUSTSTATUS -
A                                         CUSTOMERP)
A   42                                         DSPATR(RI)
A                                      6 45'(Can only be ''A'' or ''I'')'
A                                      7  3'3 .............'
A                                      7 25'Customer Name:'
A          CUSTNM    R       B   7 41REFFLD(RCUSTOMER/CUSTNAME CU-
A                                         STOMERP)
A                                             CHECK(LC)
A   43                                         DSPATR(RI PC)
A                                      8  3'4 .............'
A                                      8 24'Address Line 1:'
A          CUSTA1    R       B   8 41REFFLD(RCUSTOMER/CUSTADR1 CU-
A                                         STOMERP)
A                                             CHECK(LC)
A                                      9  3'5 .............'
A                                      9 24'Address Line 2:'
A          CUSTA2    R       B   9 41REFFLD(RCUSTOMER/CUSTADR2 CU-
A                                         STOMERP)
A                                             CHECK(LC)
A                                     10  3'6 .............'
A                                     10 34'City:'
A          CUSTCTY   R       B  10 41REFFLD(RCUSTOMER/CUSTCITY CU-
A                                         STOMERP)
A                                             CHECK(LC)
A   46                                         DSPATR(RI PC)
A                                     11  3'7 .............'
A                                     11 33'State:'
A          CUSTSTA   R       B  11 41REFFLD(RCUSTOMER/CUSTSTATE C-
A                                         USTOMERP)
A   47                                         DSPATR(RI PC)
A                                     12  3'8 .............'
A                                     12 30'Zip Code:'
A          CUSTZP    R       B  12 41REFFLD(RCUSTOMER/CUSTZIP CUS-
A                                         TOMERP)
A   48                                         DSPATR(RI PC)
A          CUSTZPE   R       B  12 47REFFLD(RCUSTOMER/CUSTZEXT CU-
A                                         STOMERP)
A   48                                         DSPATR(RI)
A                                     14  3'9 .............'
A                                     14 26'Credit Limit:'
A          CUSTCRL   R       B  14 41REFFLD(RCUSTOMER/CUSTCRLIMT -
A                                         CUSTOMERP)
A                                             EDTCDE(1)
A                                     15  2'10 .............'
A                                     15 22'Telephone Number:'
A          CUSTAC    R       B  15 41REFFLD(RCUSTOMER/CUSTAREACD -
A                                         CUSTOMERP)
A                                             EDTCDE(4)
A   50                                         DSPATR(RI PC)
A          CUSTPHN   R       B  15 45REFFLD(RCUSTOMER/CUSTPHONE C-
A                                         USTOMERP)
A                                             EDTWRD('   -   ')
A   50                                         DSPATR(RI)
A                                     17  2'11 .............'
A                                     17 28'Begin Date:'
```

*Continued*

```
A                 CUSTMON    R      B 17 41REFFLD(RCUSTOMER/CUSTDATMON -
A                                           CUSTOMERP)
A                                        EDTCDE(4)
A    51                                  DSPATR(RI PC)
A                 CUSTDAY    R      B 17 44REFFLD(RCUSTOMER/CUSTDATDAY -
A                                           CUSTOMERP)
A                                        EDTCDE(4)
A    51                                  DSPATR(RI)
A                 CUSTYR     R      B 17 47REFFLD(RCUSTOMER/CUSTDATYR C-
A                                           USTOMERP)
A                                        EDTCDE(4)
A    51                                  DSPATR(RI)
A                                   17 54'(MM DD YYYY)'
A                                   23  9'F3 = Exit'
A                                   23 23'F8 = Write new record'
A                                   23 48'Enter = Edit data'
A*
A* Message subfile records
A*
A                 R MSGRCD                 SFL
A                                          TEXT('Subfile Message')
A                                          SFLMSGRCD(24)
A                 MSGKEY                    SFLMSGKEY
A                 PGMQ                      SFLPGMQ(10)
A                 R MSGCTL                  SFLCTL(MSGRCD)
A                                           OVERLAY
A    N39                                    SFLDSP
A    N39                                    SFLDSPCTL
A    N39                                    SFLINZ
A    N39                                    SFLEND
A                                           SFLSIZ(0002)
A                                           SFLPAG(0001)
A                 PGMQ                      SFLPGMQ(10)
```

Listing B-10: DDS for the customer data entry display file

```
Ctl-Opt option(*srcstmt);
Dcl-F Cstdatent workstn indds(Inds);
Dcl-F CustomerP keyed;

Dcl-DS * PSDS;
  Pgmq Char(10) Pos(1);
End-DS;

Dcl-ds Inds;
   Exit ind pos(3);
   Write_Rec ind pos(8);
   Cust_Num_Err ind pos(41);
   Status_Err ind pos(42);
   Name_Err ind pos(43);
   City_Err ind pos(46);
   State_Err ind pos(47);
   Zip_Err ind pos(48);
   Phone_Err ind pos(50);
   Date_Err ind pos(51);
End-ds;
```

```
Dcl-s State_Ary Char(2) Dim(50) CTdata Perrcd(10);
Dcl-s Date8 packed(8:0);
Dcl-s Workdate date;
Dcl-s Work_Num packed(5:0);
Dcl-s Err_Write ind;
Dcl-s wkzipc packed(5:0);
Dcl-s wkzipec Packed(4:0);
Dcl-s msgid Char(7);
Dcl-s lineno Char(2);

Dcl-Pr CLSend Extpgm('SENDMSG');
  msgid Char(7);
  lineno Char(2);
End-Pr;
Dcl-Pr CLClear Extpgm('CLEARMSG');
End-Pr;

    // Main procedure
  Dou Exit;
  Write Msgctl;                      // Write Subfile Control
  Exfmt RCstdatent;                  // Display entry panel
  If not exit;
    Exsr ClearMessages;
    Exsr Clear_Inds;
    Chain Custnum CustomerP;         // Check customer number
    If %found(CustomerP);
      Msgid = 'DTA0101';
      Lineno = '1';
      Exsr SendaMsg;
      Cust_Num_Err = *On;            // Customer number error
      Err_write = *On;
    Else;
      Clear Rcustomer;               // Clear DB record
      CustNumber = Custnum;
    Endif;

    If Custstat = 'A' or             // Check status
       Custstat = 'I';
      Custstatus = Custstat;
    Else;
      Msgid = 'DTA0102';
      Lineno = '2';
      Exsr SendaMsg;
      Status_Err = *On;              // Status error
      Err_write = *On;
    Endif;

    If CustNM = *Blank;              // Name
      Msgid = 'DTA0103';
      Lineno = '3';
      Exsr SendaMsg;
      Name_Err = *On;
      Err_write = *On;
    Else;
      CustNM = %trim(CustNM);
      CustName = %trim(CustNM);
    Endif;
```

*Continued*

```
CustAdr1 = %trim(CustA1);       // Address Line 1
CustA1   = %trim(CustA1);       // Address Line 1
CustAdr2 = %trim(CustA2);       // Address Line 2
CustA2   = %trim(CustA2);       // Address Line 2

If Custcty = *Blank;
  Msgid = 'DTA0104';
  Lineno = '6';
  Exsr SendaMsg;
  City_Err = *On;
  Err_write = *On;
Else;
  CustCity = %trim(CustCty);
  CustCty = %trim(CustCty);
Endif;

If %lookup(CustSta:State_Ary:1) = *zero;
  Msgid = 'DTA0105';
  Lineno = '7';
  Exsr SendaMsg;
  State_Err = *On;
  Err_write = *On;
Else;
  CustState = CustSta;
Endif;

Exsr Check_zip;          // Check zip code & extension in subr

Custcrlimt = Custcrl;  // Credit Limit

If Custac < 99 or Custphn < 1000000;
  Msgid = 'DTA0107';
  Lineno = '10';
  Exsr SendaMsg;
  Phone_Err = *On;
  Err_write = *On;
Else;
  CustAreaCD = CustAC;
  CustPhone  = CustPhn;
Endif;

Date8 = CustMon * 1000000 + CustDay * 10000 + CustYr;
Monitor;  // Check date conversion
Workdate = %date(Date8:*usa);
On-Error *All;
  Msgid = 'DTA0108';
  Lineno = '11';
  Exsr SendaMsg;
  Date_Err  = *On;
  Err_write = *On;
EndMon;
If not Date_Err;
  CustDatMon = CustMon;
  CustDatDay = CustDay;
  CustDatYr  = CustYr;
Endif;

If not Err_Write and Write_Rec;  // Write new Cust Record
  Write Rcustomer;
Endif;
```

```
        Endif;
      Enddo;
      *Inlr = *on;

      Begsr Clear_Inds;
      Clear Cust_Num_Err;
      Clear Status_Err;
      Clear Name_Err;
      Clear City_Err;
      Clear State_Err;
      Clear Zip_Err;
      Clear Phone_Err;
      Clear Date_Err;
      Clear Err_Write;
      Endsr;

      Begsr Check_Zip;
      Monitor;
      Work_Num = %int(CustZp);
      If Custzpe <> *blank;
        Work_Num = %int(Custzpe);
      Endif;
      On-Error *all;
        Msgid = 'DTA0106';
        Lineno = '8';
        Exsr SendaMsg;
        Zip_Err = *On;
        Err_Write = *On;
      EndMon;
      If Not Zip_Err;
        WkZipc  = %int(CustZp);
        Custzip = %editc(WkZipc:'X');
        Custzp  = %editc(WkZipc:'X');
        If Custzpe <> *blank;
          WkZipec = %int(CustZpe);
          Custzext = %editc(WkZipec:'X');
          Custzpe  = %editc(WkZipec:'X');
        Endif;
      Endif;
      Endsr;

      Begsr Sendamsg;
      Callp CLSend(MsgID:Lineno); // Call CL Pgm
      Endsr;

      Begsr ClearMessages;
      Callp CLClear();              // Call CL Pgm
      Endsr;
**
ALAKAZARCACOCTDEFLGA
HIIDILINIAKSKYLAMEMD
MAMIMNMSMOMTNENVNHNJ
NMNYNCNDOHOKORPARISC
SDTNTXUTVTVAWAWVWIWY
```

*Listing B-11: Customer data entry RPG IV program*

```
A100XXXC                      Customer Data Entry                    3/14/15
JIM                                                                 14:30:48

   1 .......             Customer Number:      600

   2 .......                      Status:  E   (Can only be 'A' or 'I')
   3 .......             Customer Name:  Jones and Smith, Inc.
   4 .......             Address Line 1:  225 Main St.
   5 .......             Address Line 2:
   6 .......                       City:  Madison
   7 .......                      State:  WI
   8 .......                   Zip Code:  53703 2811

   9 .......              Credit Limit:  50,000.00
  10 .......           Telephone Number:  608 555-6666

  11 .......                 Begin Date:   9 16 2008   (MM DD YYYY)




           F3 = Exit     F8 = Write new record    Enter = Edit data
         Line 2: Status value entered not 'A' or 'I'
```

Listing B-12: Customer Data Entry error display

```
0001.00 /****************************************************************/
0002.00 /* PROGRAM NAME - CLEARMSG                                      */
0003.00 /* DESCRIPTION  - CLEAR PROGRAM MESSAGE QUEUE                   */
0004.00 /* COMMENT      -                                               */
0005.00 /****************************************************************/
0006.00          PGM
0007.00
0008.00          RMVMSG      PGMQ(*PRV) CLEAR(*ALL)
0009.00
0010.00          ENDPGM
```

Listing B-13: CL program CLEARMSG

```
0001.00 /*****************************************************************/
0002.00 /* PROGRAM NAME  : SENDMSG                                       */
0003.00 /* DESCRIPTION   : SEND A MESSAGE TO A PROGRAM MESSAGE QUEUE     */
0004.00 /* COMMENT       :                                              */
0005.00 /*****************************************************************/
0006.00          PGM           PARM(&MSGID &MSGDATA)
0007.00
0008.00          DCL           VAR(&MSGID) TYPE(*CHAR) LEN(7)
0009.00          DCL           VAR(&MSGDATA) TYPE(*CHAR) LEN(2)
0010.00
0011.00          SNDPGMMSG     MSGID(&MSGID) MSGF(DEMSGF) MSGDTA(&MSGDATA) +
0012.00                          TOPGMQ(*PRV)
0013.00
                 ENDPGM
```

*Listing B-14: CL program SENDMSG*

```
Message ID   Severity   Message Text
DTA0101         0       Line &1: Customer Number already in Use
DTA0102         0       Line &1: Status value entered not 'A' or 'I'
DTA0103         0       Line &1: Customer Name cannot be blank
DTA0104         0       Line &1: City cannot be all blanks
DTA0105         0       Line &1: Invalid state abbreviation entered
DTA0106         0       Line &1: Zip code entered is invalid
DTA0107         0       Line &1: Must enter valid 3 digit area code and 7
                                 digit phone number
DTA0108         0       Line &1: Invalid Date entered
```

*Listing B-15: Message file contents*

# Sales Report Program

The sales report program produces a sales report with several level breaks.
Listing B-16 shows what the sales report produced looks like. Listing B-17
shows the DDS for the printer file. Listing B-18 shows the RPG IV program.

Martin Widget Company
Sales Report for Sales Person    30

| State | Year | Month | Day | Customer Number | Invoice Number | Invoice Amount | Open Amount |
|-------|------|-------|-----|-----------------|----------------|---------------|-------------|
| IL | 2013 | 12 | 30 | 500 | 9051 | 1,000.00 | .00 |
|  | 2013 | 12 |  | Total for Month: |  | 1,000.00 | .00 |
| IL |  |  |  | Total for State: |  | 1,000.00 | .00 |
|  | 2013 |  |  | Total for Year: |  | 1,000.00 | .00 |
| AL | 2014 | 1 | 15 | 100 | 10010 | 2,000.00 | 2,000.00 |
| AL | 2014 | 1 | 20 | 100 | 10050 | 1,500.00 | 1,500.00 |
|  | 2014 | 1 |  | Total for Month: |  | 3,500.00 | 3,500.00 |
| AL | 2014 | 2 | 7 | 100 | 10100 | 7,300.00 | 5,500.00 |
|  | 2014 | 2 |  | Total for Month: |  | 7,300.00 | 5,500.00 |
| AL |  |  |  | Total for State: |  | 10,800.00 | 9,000.00 |
| CO | 2014 | 1 | 16 | 200 | 10011 | 3,000.00 | 2,500.00 |
|  | 2014 | 1 |  | Total for Month: |  | 3,000.00 | 2,500.00 |
| CO |  |  |  | Total for State: |  | 3,000.00 | 2,500.00 |
| ME | 2014 | 1 | 16 | 300 | 10012 | 1,000.00 | .00 |
|  | 2014 | 1 |  | Total for Month: |  | 1,000.00 | .00 |
| ME |  |  |  | Total for State: |  | 1,000.00 | .00 |
| NH | 2014 | 1 | 16 | 400 | 10013 | 500.00 | 500.00 |
| NH | 2014 | 1 | 17 | 400 | 10014 | 7,030.00 | 5,000.00 |
|  | 2014 | 1 |  | Total for Month: |  | 7,530.00 | 5,500.00 |
| NH |  |  |  | Total for State: |  | 7,530.00 | 5,500.00 |

```
===============================================================================
Page 2                              Martin Widget Company
                            Sales Report for Sales Person   30

                            Customer Invoice              Invoice              Open
State Year Month Day        Number   Number               Amount              Amount
      2014                  Total for Year:             22,330.00           17,000.00


                            Total for Person:           23,330.00           17,000.00


===============================================================================
Page 3                              Martin Widget Company
                            Sales Report for Sales Person   40

                            Customer Invoice              Invoice              Open
State Year Month Day        Number   Number               Amount              Amount

 IA   2013  12   30           175     9053                730.00                .00

 IA   2013  12   30           175     9055                917.00                .00

      2013  12              Total for Month:            1,647.00                .00

 IA                         Total for State:            1,647.00                .00

 MN   2014   1   21           600    10060               145.00              145.00

 MN   2014   1   22           600    10061               850.00              200.00

      2014   1              Total for Month:              995.00              345.00

 MN                         Total for State:              995.00              345.00

 OH   2014   1   17           250    10015               325.00              325.00

 OH                         Total for State:              325.00              325.00

      2014                  Total for Year:             1,320.00              670.00


                            Total for Person:           2,967.00              670.00
```

*Listing B-16: Sample sales report*

```
     *-----------------------------------------------------------------
     *--- Printer file:  SALESRPT1
     *---
     *--- Purpose:  Print Sales Person Report by Month, State, and Yr
     *---
     *-----------------------------------------------------------------
     A                                         REF(CUSTSALES)
     *-
     A           R HEADINGS
     *-
     A                                       4 31'Martin Widget Company'
     A                                       4  1'Page'
     A                                       4  6PAGNBR EDTCDE(Z)
     *-
     A                                       5 25'Sales Report for Sales-
     A                                          Person'
     A           SAVEPERSONR                 5 54EDTCDE(J) REFFLD(SLPERSON)
     *-
     A                                       8 23'Customer'
     A                                       8 32'Invoice'
     A                                       8 52'Invoice'
     A                                       8 75'Open'
     *-
     A                                       9  1'State'
     A                                       9  7'Year'
     A                                       9 12'Month'
     A                                       9 18'Day'
     A                                       9 23'Number'
     A                                       9 32'Number'
     A                                       9 53'Amount'
     A                                       9 73'Amount'
     *-----------------------------------------------------------------
     *-
     A           R DETAIL
     *-
     A                                         SPACEB(2)
     A           SLSTATE    R                 2
     A           SLIYY      R                 7
     A           SLIMM      R                13EDTCDE(Z)
     A           SLIDD      R                18EDTCDE(Z)
     A           SLCUSNUM   R                23EDTCDE(Z)
     A           SLINVNUM   R                32EDTCDE(Z)
     A           SLIAMT     R                47EDTCDE(J)
     A           SLOAMT     R                67EDTCDE(J)
     *-----------------------------------------------------------------
     A           R TOTMON
     A                                         SPACEB(2)
     A                                         SPACEA(1)
     A           SAVEYEAR   R                 7REFFLD(SLIYY)
     A           SAVEMONTH  R                13REFFLD(SLIMM) EDTCDE(Z)
     A                                        23'Total for Month:'
     A           TL1IAMT      11  2          45EDTCDE(J)
     A           TL1OAMT      11  2          65EDTCDE(J)
     *-----------------------------------------------------------------
     A           R TOTSTATE
     A                                         SPACEB(2)
     A                                         SPACEA(1)
     A           SAVESTATE  R                 2REFFLD(SLSTATE)
     A                                        23'Total for State:'
     A           TL2IAMT      11  2          45EDTCDE(J)
```

```
A               TL2OAMT      11  2    65EDTCDE(J)
 *-----------------------------------------------------------------
A          R TOTYEAR
A                                    SPACEB(2)
A                                    SPACEA(1)
A               SAVEYEAR  R           7REFFLD(SLIYY)
A                                    23'Total for Year:'
A               TL3IAMT      11  2   45EDTCDE(J)
A               TL3OAMT      11  2   65EDTCDE(J)
 *-----------------------------------------------------------------
A          R TOTPERSON
A                                    SPACEB(3)
A                                    23'Total for Person:'
A               TL4IAMT      11  2   45EDTCDE(J)
A               TL4OAMT      11  2   65EDTCDE(J)
```

*Listing B-17: DDS for sales report printer file*

```
//----------------------------------------------------------------
// Program name: SalesRpt1
//
// Purpose:     Print detail sales and totals for each salesperson
//              by year, state, and month.
//
//----------------------------------------------------------------
//  Define the files to be used

Dcl-F CustSls11 keyed;
Dcl-F SalesRpt1 Printer OFLIND(Overflow);
Dcl-s Overflow ind;

// Main Procedure

Read CustSls11;

If not %eof(CustSls11);

  SavePerson = SLperson;
  Write Headings;

Endif;

SaveState = SlState;
SaveYear  = Sliyy;
SaveMonth = Slimm;

Dow not %eof(CustSls11);  // Do while not at eof

  If SlPerson <> Saveperson;
    Exsr Check_Overflow;
    Exsr Month_break;

    Exsr Check_Overflow;
    Exsr State_break;
    Exsr Check_Overflow;
    Exsr Year_break;
    Exsr Check_Overflow;
```

*Continued*

```
      Exsr Person_break;
      Write Headings;
   Endif;

   If SliYY <> SaveYear;
      Exsr Check_Overflow;
      Exsr Month_break;

      Exsr Check_Overflow;
      Exsr State_break;

      Exsr Check_Overflow;
      Exsr Year_break;
   Endif;

   If SlState <> SaveState;
      Exsr Check_Overflow;
      Exsr Month_break;

      Exsr Check_Overflow;
      Exsr State_break;
   Endif;

   If SliMM <> SaveMonth;
      Exsr Check_Overflow;
      Exsr Month_break;
   Endif;

   Exsr Check_Overflow;
   Write DETAIL;         // Print customer detail

   Exsr AccumDet;

   Read CustSlsl1;       // Read next record in the file

 Enddo;

 Exsr Month_Break;
 Exsr State_Break;
 Exsr Year_Break;
 Exsr Person_Break;

 *Inlr = *On;           // End program

 //---------------------------------------------------------------
 Begsr AccumDet;

 TL1iamt += Sliamt;
 TL1oamt += Sloamt;

 Endsr;
 //---------------------------------------------------------------
 Begsr Month_Break;

 TL2iamt += Tl1iamt;
 TL2oamt += Tl1oamt;

 Write TotMon;
```

```
          Clear Tl1iamt;
          Clear Tl1oamt;
          SaveMonth = Slimm;
          Endsr;
          //----------------------------------------------------------------
          Begsr State_Break;

          TL3iamt += Tl2iamt;
          TL3oamt += Tl2oamt;

          Write TotState;

          Clear Tl2iamt;
          Clear Tl2oamt;
          SaveState = SlState;

          Endsr;
          //----------------------------------------------------------------
          Begsr Year_Break;

          TL4iamt += Tl3iamt;
          TL4oamt += Tl3oamt;

          Write TotYear;

          Clear Tl3iamt;
          Clear Tl3oamt;
          SaveYear = SliYY;

          Endsr;
          //----------------------------------------------------------------
          Begsr Person_break;

          Write TotPerson;

          Clear Tl4iamt;
          Clear Tl4oamt;

          Saveperson = Slperson;
          Endsr;
          //----------------------------------------------------------------
          Begsr Check_Overflow;
            If Overflow;              // Check for and handle overflow
            // If true, print headings and reset overflow indicator
              Write Headings;
              Reset Overflow;
            Endif;
          Endsr;
```

*Listing B-18: Sales report RPG IV program*

# C

# Free-Format Alternatives for Fixed-Format Operations

| Fixed-format operation | Description | Free-format alternative |
|---|---|---|
| Add | Add | Use the + (plus) or += accumulation operator in an assignment expression or an Eval operation. |
| Adddur | Add duration | Use + or += with the %Months, %Days, or %Years built-in function. |
| Alloc | Allocate storage | Use the %Alloc built-in function. |
| And*xx* | And | Use the And operator within the comparison expression. |
| Bitoff | Set bits off | Use the %Bitand and %Bitnot built-in functions. |
| Biton | Set bits on | Use the %Bitor built-in function. |

| Fixed-format operation | Description | Free-format alternative |
|---|---|---|
| Cab*xx* | Compare and branch | Use loop interrupters (e.g., Iter, Leave, LeaveSr, Return). |
| Call | Call a program | Use the CallP operation, and supply a prototype with the ExtPgm keyword. |
| CallB | Call a bound procedure | Use the CallP operation, and supply a prototype with the ExtProc keyword. |
| Cas*xx* | Conditionally invoke subroutine | Use an If/Elseif/Else/Endif group or a Select/When/Other/Endsl group, and invoke subroutines using the Exsr operation. |
| Cat | Concatenate two strings | Use the + operator in an Eval expression. |
| Check | Check characters | Use the %Check built-in function. |
| CheckR | Check reverse | Use the %Checkr built-in function. |
| Comp | Compare | Use If with <, <=, =, >=, >, or <> operators in the comparison expression. |
| Define | Field definition | Use the Like or DTAARA keyword on the appropriate definition specification. |
| Div | Divide | Use the / (forward slash) or /= assignment operator on an assignment expression, or use the %Div built-in function (integer part of quotient only). |
| Do | Do | Use the For operator. |
| Dou*xx* | Do until | Use the Dou operation. |
| Dow*xx* | Do while | Use the Dow operation. |
| End | End (generic) | Use a specific End*xx* operation (e.g., Endif, Enddo, Endsl). |
| Endcs | End a Cas*xx* group | Use the appropriate End*xx* for an If or Select group that replaces Cas. |
| Extrct | Extract date/time/timestamp | Use the %Subdt built-in function. |
| Goto | Go to | Use structured programming with loop interrupters (e.g., Iter, Leave, LeaveSr, Return). |
| If*xx* | If | Use the If operation and an expression. |

| Fixed-format operation | Description | Free-format alternative |
|---|---|---|
| Kfld | Define parts of a key | Use "in-line" key fields or the %Kds built-in function for Chain, Set, and others. |
| Klist | Define a composite key | Use "in-line" key fields or the %Kds built-in function for Chain, Set, and others. |
| Lookup | Look up a table or array element | For table lookup, use the %Tlookup built-in or its variations. For array lookup, use the %Lookup built-in or its variations. |
| MHHZO | Move high to high zone | Use the %Bitand and %Bitor built-in functions. |
| MHLZO | Move high to low zone | Use the %Bitand and %Bitor built-in functions. |
| MLHZO | Move low to high zone | Use the %Bitand and %Bitor built-in functions. |
| MLLZO | Move low to low zone | Use the %Bitand and %Bitor built-in functions. |
| Move | Move (right adjust data) | Use Eval or EvalR operations with many possible built-in functions, depending on the circumstances: %Char, %Int, %Date, %Dec, %Time, %Uns, and others (see **Chapter 10**). |
| MoveA | Move array | Use character-management built-in functions or the %Subarr built-in function (see **Chapter 10**). |
| MoveL | Move left (left adjust data) | Use the Eval operator with many possible built-in functions, depending on the circumstances: %Char, %Int, %Date, %Dec, %Time, %Uns, and others (see **Chapter 10**). |
| Mult | Multiply | Use the * (multiplication) or *= accumulation operator in an assignment expression or Eval operation. |
| Mvr | Move remainder | Use the %Rem built-in function. |
| Occur | Set/Get occurrence of a data structure | Use the %Occur built-in function. |
| Or*xx* | Or | Use the Or operator within the comparison expression. |

| Fixed-format operation | Description | Free-format alternative |
|---|---|---|
| Parm | Identify parameters | Specify parameters on a prototype or procedure interface in definition specifications. |
| Plist | Identify a parameter list | Specify parameters on a prototype or procedure interface in definition specifications. |
| Realloc | Reallocate storage with new length | Use the %Realloc built-in function. |
| Scan | Scan string | Use the %Scan built-in function. |
| Setoff | Set indicator off | Use an assignment expression to set off named or numbered indicators. |
| Seton | Set indicator on | Use assignment expression to set on named or numbered indicators. |
| Shtdn | Shut down | Use the %Shut built-in function. |
| Sqrt | Square root | Use the %Sqrt built-in function. |
| Sub | Subtract | Use a – (minus) or –= assignment operator in an assignment expression or Eval operation. |
| Subdur | Subtract duration | Use the – or –= operator with date or time built-in functions %Days, %Months, %Years, %Hours, %Minutes, or %Seconds, or use the %Diff built-in function. |
| Subst | Substring | Use the %Subst built-in function. |
| Tag | Tag (for Goto) | Use structured programming and loop interrupters (e.g., Iter, Leave, LeaveSr, Return). |
| TestB | Test bit | Use the %Bitand built-in function. |
| TestN | Test numeric | Use a Monitor group with On-error around the use of the field that may not be numeric. |
| TestZ | Test zone | Use the %Bitand built-in function and X'F0' to narrow focus to the zone. |
| Time | Retrieve time and date | Use the %Time built-in function to get the current time; use %Date to get the current date. Use %Timestamp to get both the date and time. Use %Dec or %Char to convert these values to decimal or character. |

| Fixed-format operation | Description | Free-format alternative |
|---|---|---|
| When*xx* | When true then select | Use the When operator with an expression. |
| Xfoot | Sum the elements of an array | Use the %Xfoot built-in function. |
| Xlate | Translate | Use the %Xlate built-in function. |
| Z-Add | Zero and add | Use an assignment expression or an Eval operation. |
| Z-Sub | Zero and subtract | Use an assignment expression or an Eval operation. |

# Index